Quantum Jumps

Also by Cynthia Sue Larson

Aura Advantage
RealityShifters Guide to High Energy Money
Karen Kimball and the Dream Weaver's Web
Reality Shifts

Quantum Jumps

An Extraordinary Science of Happiness and Prosperity

Cynthia Sue Larson

QUANTUM JUMPS
An Extraordinary Science of Happiness and Prosperity

The word 'quantum' was coined in 1900 by the German physicist Max Planck who clearly understood the implications of this scientific breakthrough. It has taken a century for the rest of the world to catch up with him, but the 'Quantum Age' has finally arrived. Cynthia Sue Larson understands its implications for our everyday lives—for how we can make wiser decisions, how we can relate better to other people, how we can manage our careers more effectively, how we can use our dreams to provide insights, and even how we can use 'quantum jumping' for self-healing. Larson's readers might start reading this remarkable book thinking that theoretical physics is beyond their comprehension. But the examples, the exercises, and the lucid writing style will not only prove them wrong but will shift their view of reality and the role they can play in constructing it.
— Stanley Krippner, co-author, *Personal Mythology*

Multiverse, alternate realities and quantum physics have taken root in American consciousness. We know that the universe is bigger and more mysterious than we can imagine. Cynthia Sue Larson is the first writer to provide a manual to allow us to experience the truth of the new physics. Better yet, Cynthia shows us how to manifest new positive realities that are surrounding us. She shows us what to do to make our Quantum Jump to these higher orders of reality. Her work is an amazing achievement and a stellar addition to the field of mind-body research.
— Dr. Donald "Rock" Schnell, author, *Young for Life*

QUANTUM JUMPS
An Extraordinary Science of Happiness and Prosperity

The twenty-first century will be remembered as the era in which quantum physics, biology, and consciousness started shaking hands. We now know that 'quantum' is no longer limited to the invisible, subatomic realm, but involves our everyday world and our own mind. Cynthia Sue Larson's *QUANTUM JUMPS* is a daring, adventuresome, delightful romp in this territory. This book proves that physics can be fun. Written in sparkling, clear language, *QUANTUM JUMPS* will inspire anyone toward a more fulfilling, effective, and happier life. Highly recommended!
— Larry Dossey, M.D., author *The Power of Premonitions* and *One Mind*

In *QUANTUM JUMPS*, Cynthia Sue Larson illustrates how "quantum jumping" can greatly transform our everyday lives, bringing fresh new perspectives and clarity through one of our most natural gifts—the imagination. We are expertly guided into the knowledge that through imagining a more meaningful life and quietly meditating to break free from discursive thoughts that often impede our progress, we can envision and access or 'quantum jump' into a new paradigm of infinite possibilities and reconnect with the reality that we are connected to an eternal infinite source. This book is well written, easy to follow, and I highly recommend it to everyone who is seeking ways to live a more meaningful life.
— Annamaria Hemingway, Ph.D., author of *Practicing Conscious Living and Dying, Myths of the Afterlife, Immortal Yearnings*, and *Nature's Living Legacy*

QUANTUM JUMPS
An Extraordinary Science of Happiness and Prosperity

Cynthia Sue Larson has an exceptional gift of putting in writing what most of us outside of the physics world would categorize as unknowable. Her newest work, *QUANTUM JUMPS* is no exception. Through science, stories and Q&A dialogue, Cynthia not only provides the reader with an understanding of quantum concepts, but also practical ways to jump into new realities. Cynthia demonstrates that we are the ones who determine "How good can it get?" through our beliefs, attitudes and actions. This book is one you will want to keep and return to as you reflect deeper on the concepts. I highly recommend *QUANTUM JUMPS* to all who desire to move out of "stuckness" and jump into a state of well-being!
— Jennifer Reich, PhD, RN, author of *States of Faith: Poems of Healing*

QUANTUM JUMPS
An Extraordinary Science of Happiness and Prosperity

Cynthia Larson's new book *QUANTUM JUMPS* offers her latest insights into using the quantum metaphor to explain a number of human experiences that go beyond what we would normally call "normal." She writes with clarity, vision, and offers hope and encouragement to those who often fear such experiences that go beyond accepted norms of existence.
— Fred Alan Wolf, aka Dr. Quantum

Cynthia Sue Larson's signature ability to convey the exquisite elegance of the spectrum of reality is replete in this volume called *QUANTUM JUMPS*! A brilliant blend of science and spirituality, possible and probable, *QUANTUM JUMPS* will catapult the reader into a whole new view of potential and remind us that we've always occupied this fantastic world of quantum reality, but it is now that we must act upon it! I highly recommend this delightful book to anyone needing a verifiable record of the miraculous, mystical and magnificent. You will not want to put this book down!
— Alexis Brooks, radio show host and author of *Conscious Musings: A Collection of Contemplations about Life and Potentiality*

QUANTUM JUMPS
An Extraordinary Science of Happiness and Prosperity

Printing History: First trade paper edition 2013

RealityShifters®
P.O. Box 7393
Berkeley, CA 94707-7393
www.realityshifters.com

Copyright © 2013 by Cynthia Sue Larson
Illustrated by Alina Larson
Cover art by Tessala Larson

ISBN-13: 9780971934955
ISBN-10: 0971934959

CONTENTS

Acknowledgements

I am deeply grateful for and offer heartfelt thanks to all my family, colleagues and friends whose unwavering support made all the difference, and whose confidence in me and my ideas helped make this book a reality.

I extend very special thanks to PMH Atwater, Cleve Backster, John Cramer, Dr. Larry Dossey, Stanley Krippner, Bruce Lipton, Lynne McTaggart, Jeff Mishlove, Edgar Mitchell, Dean Radin, William Shatner, In Hyuk Suh, William Tiller, and Fred Alan Wolf, whose inspiration, support, and advice made this book possible.

"Everything in the universe
is within you.
Ask all from yourself."
— *Rumi*

Welcome to the Quantum Age

A new Quantum Age is upon us, and with new quantum technologies arrives a new science of instant transformation. In a moment you can become healthier, smarter, more confident, happier, more outgoing, more effective, more energetic, more tenacious, in better relationships, with better vision and willpower. In this new Quantum Age, our experience of reality is transformed when we acknowledge we are all connected—and that at any given moment, there exists an infinite number of possibilities.

When making quantum jumps to a reality you enjoy, rather than manifesting or bringing something into your life, you *become* the change you wish to see in the world. Recent studies in the fields of psychology, sociology, and medicine show positive results for those who "fake it 'til they make it," by adopting confident body postures, dressing for success, and benefitting from placebo pills, surgeries, and subliminal cues. We become happier, smarter, and more confident by doing a few straightforward things that signal to ourselves that we already possess these beneficial qualities. Simply focusing our attention more consistently in areas we'd most like to experience further enhances already positive results.

Schrödinger's Cat is Out of the Box

Austrian physicist Erwin Schrödinger's cat is a famous example of how seemingly bizarre quantum behavior can affect a living being. Schrödinger devised an ingenious thought experiment in which a cat's very life depends upon a single subatomic particle. In this thought experiment, a cat is enclosed in a sealed compartment together with a glass vial of poison gas that is controlled by a mechanism that can be randomly triggered by an atom of radioactive material. When the radioactive material decays, the mechanism is triggered, thus breaking the glass vial and killing the cat. In the world of classical physics, we would expect that if we peeked inside of the box, we would find that our experimental cat was either alive or dead. In the world of quantum physics, Schrödinger's cat can be alive or dead—and it can also potentially exist in a state of being both alive *and* dead at the same time. Being both alive and dead at the same time is an example of what's called a superposition of states. Observers would never actually see an alive-and-dead cat, yet behavior of quantum particles clearly indicates that such superposition of states are common occurrences on the microscopic scale.

Thanks to the race to build quantum computers, harnessing the remarkable power of quantum behaviors on a macroscopic scale, Schrödinger's thought experiment is much more than just an amusing side note in introductory physics classes. The race to build quantum computers is now propelling humanity into a new world of fuzzy logic, probability, and quantum optimization. Rather than relying on the familiar binary bits of zeros and ones, quantum computers depend upon qubits— quantum bits—which exist in a blurry superposition of states that can be both 0 and 1 at the same time. Quantum computers will tackle complex problems that our current classical computers can't address, such as weather-forecasting problems involving multiple variables influencing one another.

We can tell that we've officially entered the Quantum Age when we see how quantum effects are no longer limited exclusively to the realm of the very small. At this extraordinary time in human history, physicists are demonstrating quantum physics behavior at room temperature with larger-than-quantum objects. The kind of quantum behavior Albert Einstein once called *spooky action at a distance* can now be observed at room temperature in objects we can see with the naked eye and hold in our hands. Scientists are now observing quantum behavior once thought to be relegated exclusively to submicroscopic realms such as entanglement, superposition of states, coherence, tunneling, and teleportation in our everyday world at a very human level. New interdisciplinary branches of science are springing forth that invite us to recognize our quantum biological nature, harness the phenomenal power of the placebo, and discover how we can take positive actions to change our reality.

Quantum Computers Change Our Lives

When you first see the rather plain boxy black cube that is the D-Wave Two, you might not suspect that tens of millions of dollars were spent developing this first commercial quantum computer jointly purchased by Google and the Ames Research Center. The D-Wave Two with its 512 qubit processing power is an early front-runner quantum computer that portends a generation of new things to come. Thanks to quantum superposition of states, quantum qubits contain information in all possible states, and entangled qubits thus have the capability to efficiently compute optimal solutions for some of the most complex, vexing, and currently unsolvable problems known to mankind. Quantum computing will likely change everything from the way the stock market functions to every aspect of information security, weather forecasting, and trend analysis.

My Industrial Age counterpart would have typeset a book like this using mechanical typewriters and printing presses that could print thousands of books in a period of months. I'm now composing these sentences using word processing software running on a laptop computer that allows me to publish my book across a wide variety of media platforms accommodating nearly infinite digital and paperback book demand. In the coming Quantum Age, every aspect of writing will be transformed, with a symbiosis between writers and readers in ways we can only begin to imagine. Thanks to quantum computing, my future counterpart's software will be able to anticipate what she is about to write as ideas occur to her, "mind melding" with her in ways that speed the typing of her words into chapters, so whole sentences spring into being as the first words are composed, and entire sections of her book come together simultaneously. Far more than simply anticipating what the author is about to write, this new Quantum Age software will anticipate as-yet-unrealized trends, guiding the author to include areas of greatest future reader interest. Reader reactions to material will be predicted as my Quantum Age counterpart composes it, showing future popular ideas and interests before they've even arrived.

The Quantum Age Mindset

What's most amazing to me about the Quantum Age isn't so much about the quantum computers as how radically our concept of rational thinking is about to change. The seemingly simple transition from bits to qubits takes us from our westernized binary view of True-False logic into a wild and woolly realm of True, True-and-False, Not-True-Not-False, and False. We're entering a weird, wonderful world of possibilities in which we'll discover that just because we think something is a certain way doesn't mean it will stay that way, or that others will experience it that way. Our legal systems will be transformed, and historians, psychologists, sociologists, anthropologists and biologists will recognize alternate histories as being a natural part of existence. Medical professionals will learn to view spontaneous remission as a naturally occurring process, and will encourage people to adopt states of mind that facilitate quantum jumps in healing. Our views of unbiased observers and impartial judges will be forever changed as we appreciate how information can travel anywhere instantaneously, and how everyone and everything is interconnected. The Quantum Age invites us to radically transform our view of who we are and how we work, play, love, and heal in our everyday lives.

While the word "quantum" is over 100 years old, only now is there such an amazing synthesis of evidence coming together across many scientific fields and disciplines that we can begin to understand a more complete picture of ourselves and the world around us. Quantum behavior is now regularly witnessed on the macroscopic scale in laboratory research settings, rather than remaining relegated to the realm of the microscopically small. Biologists are noticing signs of quantum mechanics assisting birds and plants, as well as at work inside our bodies. The "placebo effect" mysteriously continues to grow in efficacy, demonstrating that "sham" surgery, sugar pills, and even pretend flashed subliminal test answers improve people's circumstances across a wide variety of types of situations. Over 90% of people report noticing synchronicity and coincidences, and more than half of people surveyed report seeing things moving without being touched. For the first time in history, a majority of physicists surveyed confidently assert that you and I and *every* physical thing exists in a superposition of states. In simpler terms, this means our leading experts on reality are telling us there are as many possible you's and as many possible me's as you can imagine... and then some! Social scientists and psychologists are conducting research studies that clearly show that when we behave and act *as if* we are happy, confident, healthy or in love, we *become* happy, confident, healthy and in love.

As we examine all the above seemingly disparate research areas with an eye to finding a common denominator, the point that something wonderful and amazing is going on becomes clear. We are entering an extraordinary era in which the previously dominant paradigm of material realism is giving way to a new concept of interconnectedness. No longer can we pretend that matter is all that matters, disregard nonlocal effects, or claim that we can be completely objective. We have crossed the threshold into the Quantum Age in which we know for absolute certain that everything we think of as matter also simultaneously exists in pure energy form. We know that entanglements exist between everything in existence. We know that to observe anything, no matter how discreetly, is to influence events. We know we can only ever "know" anything in terms of probabilities, rather than absolutes.

One of the most practical skills we can learn in this new Quantum Age is the art and science of quantum jumping. We are constantly involved in quantum jumping between parallel realities, though seldom consciously aware of this natural activity. In a multiverse of possibilities, only when we find we have completely different memories of events—such as recalling a different ending of a book or movie, or a completely different conversation or sequence of events—do we get an inkling of how we are moving through shifting worlds of possibility. When we notice that such alternate histories exist, we often gain our first clue that something extraordinary has transpired. Talking about and sharing memories of alternate histories, such as Nelson Mandela having died in prison many years ago, affords us a new kind of freedom as we become more consciously aware of just how much the world can change.

Nature has a marvelous way of making sure that nothing is wasted. With respect to the existence of many possible realities in co-existing parallel universes, this means that rather than living out our lives entirely in any one universe, we literally travel between worlds, quantum jumping from one reality to another. People who have spontaneous remissions of cancer or other types of disease, who suddenly come out of a coma, or who are thrown clear of a deadly automobile accident have experienced this kind of quantum jump first-hand.

Plants and animals demonstrate marvelous examples of co-existing in parallel universes by naturally testing out possibilities until finding a way through to a solution that ultimately proves best. The process of photosynthesis in plants is an excellent example of this, with plants at the cellular level trying out all possible paths when absorbing and harvesting light energy from photons until they find the most efficient route. Our noses can detect remarkably dilute fragrances despite limited olfactory receptors by virtue of vibrations of what is being smelled in a way that allows us to discern differences between isotopes of chemicals with identical shapes that smell entirely different.

The Quantum Age takes us far beyond the Information Age to a way of living in which we delight in uncertainty, thrive in entanglement, and flourish with an awareness of many possibilities. In the Quantum Age, we depend upon the fact that many possible realities coexist at every point in space and time. This new Quantum Age represents a fusion between intuitive and rational understanding of a holistic reality. While the view of an entangled, nonlocal multiverse might at first seem to be a completely modern discovery, many ancient indigenous cultures and proponents of the Hermetic worldview have long maintained that humans are born with an innate connection to the unseen essence from which all material things spring forth. By simply asking, *"How can I experience quantum effects in everyday life?",* we welcome a new, direct experience with creative energetic essence.

There is a Zen of qubit processing logic that can be more easily understood from an Eastern fourfold logic view. Rather than adopting the simple True-or-False dichotomy of classical computing bits, quantum qubits exist in the realm of such possibilities as True, False, True-and-False, and Not-True-Not-False. Such a lack of certainty in favor of optimization may seem strange at first, but this direction of mindfulness is the direction of the new Quantum Age. The Quantum Age invites us to embrace uncertainty, recognize interconnectedness, and raise our level of energy in order to experience a better way of life.

Through quantum entanglement, in which invisible connections are capable of relaying information instantaneously across great distances, we recognize a mechanism by which we can better comprehend intuition. Through quantum teleportation we see how we can sometimes travel farther in less time. Through quantum coherence we better understand synchronicity and coincidence, and through quantum superposition of states we glean insights into spontaneous remission of disease that can occur when people experience lucid dreams or near death experience states of mind.

I first wrote and talked about quantum jumps between parallel realities in the reality shifting workshops I conducted in the late 1990s. I shared information about how consciousness changes the physical world from my book, *Reality Shifts,* in its original three-ring binder form. I described reality shifts and wrote about reality shift experiences in which things appeared, disappeared, transformed and transported... as well as changes in the experience of time. The monthly RealityShifters ezine has been a free source of reality shift articles, stories, book reviews, movie reviews, and survey results since 1999. It wasn't until 2012, when the producers of the History Channel's *William Shatner's Weird or What?* TV show contacted me that I began publicly using the words "quantum" and "jumping" together in the same sentence.

My hesitation in adopting the term "quantum jumping" sprang from a conversation I had with Dr. Larry Dossey in 1998 when discussing my book, *Reality Shifts: When Consciousness Changes the Physical World.* Dr. Dossey implored, *"Please don't write another book using the word quantum. It's so over-used."* He elaborated that thanks to many peoples' runaway enthusiasm, the word 'quantum' had become almost meaninglessness through excessive use and exposure, with inadequate supporting explanation of underlying concepts. The net result has been that

11

people have become overly enamored with the word quantum, while seldom having any true knowledge of what it means.

To get a feeling for how labels provide a false sense of comprehension, consider the word 'gravity.' Most people will likely tell you that they know what gravity is—it's what makes an apple fall down to the ground from a tree, rather than float aimlessly through space, or zip up into the sky. It's what keeps our Earth revolving around our Sun. It's how we know how much we weigh, and something to keep in mind when navigating slippery surfaces. While we appreciate the general attributes of gravity, none of us can truthfully say for sure what gravity actually *is*, how it really works, or even why it exists. We might think of gravity in terms of it being one of the four fundamental known forces of nature (along with the electromagnetic force, the weak nuclear force, and the strong nuclear force), and be able to recognize equations by which we can predict interactions between various physical bodies—yet gravity essentially remains a mystery.

If we use words such as "quantum" without getting to know the underlying concepts, we run the risk of thinking we understand things while not truly comprehending them at all. It might be considered acceptable when driving cars, using computers, or talking on cell phones to use these devices without fully appreciating all that goes into making these things work, but it's important we respect the truth of what such words represent, and avoid haphazard use of language.

After a decade of mulling over Dr. Dossey's advice, in January 2013 I readdressed the matter of quantum jumping with him via email, writing, *"I'm checking in with you on my quantum jumping book not so much to get permission or approval as to find out your thoughts on the matter now, and also for any insights, ideas or observations you might wish to offer. I so deeply respect your professional opinion on this matter, and thank you in advance for whatever you feel inspired to share."*

Dr. Dossey replied,

> *"I just read your website on quantum jumping and, for what it's worth, I think it is superb. Very clear and compelling. After reading it, I realize I 'quantum jump' all the time. Our thousands of decisions on 'how to be' and 'intend' that we make in a day's time, all those bifurcations of decision points, can be conceived as quantum jumps, if I get your meaning correctly."*

Yes, this was precisely my meaning, and I'm grateful to Dr. Dossey both for his exceptionally keen grasp of this topic and his awareness that the time has come for a thorough exploration of this subject that includes scientific and historic information, as well as personal anecdotes and experiences.

This book, *Quantum Jumps,* presents a radical new paradigm—that we exist in a holographic multiverse in which we can literally jump from one parallel universe to another. Supported by distinguished sources from the fields of physics, biology, psychology, sociology and medicine, *Quantum Jumps* provides you with the means to make an immediate shift to be the change you wish to see in the world. *Quantum Jumps* is packed with real-life quantum jump examples, scientific research, simple exercises and profound insights to help you make your life the best it can be. A wealth of practical tools is provided to help you achieve real change in your life, regardless of your past history. Get ready to leap forward and become your happiest, most prosperous self, living the life of your dreams!

"I regard consciousness as fundamental. I regard matter as derivative from consciousness. We cannot get behind consciousness. Everything that we talk about, everything that we regard as existing, postulates consciousness."

— Max Planck

Chapter 1

Experiencing the
Quantum Realm

When a tornado that sounded like "a dozen freight trains" came tearing down through Ashley Clouse's Arkansas community in April 2013, she didn't hesitate for a second to follow her husband's lead out of their home to the backyard with her 19-month-old child in hand. Ashley knew that they had only a matter of minutes to find shelter from the massive oncoming storm, and their home was no longer safe. Standing atop a giant boulder, Ashley realized she had a split-second decision to make: whether to risk leaping almost ten feet straight down to safety in a natural cave under the boulder, or take extra time seeking another way down. As the storm bore down with horrifyingly destructive force, *"I just jumped off,"* Ashley said, in a move that saved her family's lives.

We sometimes encounter life-changing moments when decisions and actions made in microseconds influence large subsequent sequences of events. If Ashley had not acted so quickly, she might have lost much more than just her home and possessions that day. When we examine split-second decisions more closely, we find a physics of time and space of the very small... a world of quantum physics.

The realm of quantum particles stretches our minds as we imagine the tiniest building blocks of reality, and how necessary they are for the existence of our universe. In 1900 German physicist Max Planck, the "Father of Quantum Physics," chose the word "quantum" to describe the small, discrete packets of energy that electromagnetic radiation consists of from the Latin word, *quanta*, meaning "how great" or "how much." This seemed the perfect word to convey the essence of the most fundamental component of matter known at the time. The quest to find the tiniest particles from which all matter is composed ultimately led to the disquieting realization that at its very core, quantum particles are not so much simple matter as they are either matter or energy, consisting in a wave state. Planck once described his understanding of quantum particles thus:

> *"As a man who has devoted his whole life to the most clear headed science, to the study of matter, I can tell you as a result of my research about atoms this much: There is no matter as such. All matter originates and exists only by virtue of a force which brings the particle of an atom to vibration and holds this most minute solar system of the atom together. We must assume behind this force the existence of a conscious and intelligent mind. This mind is the matrix of all matter."*

The intrinsic mystery of quantum particles with their dual material/wave nature presented a challenge for physicists seeking ways to best measure and describe them. Physicists Ernest Rutherford gave us a nuclear model of the atom in 1911 that physicist Niels Bohr expanded to include a planetary structure with stationary energy states. Louis de Broglie broadened our view of quantum wave-particle duality by suggesting in 1923 that quantum particles of matter can also behave like energy waves.

There was fanfare and great excitement in 1986 when the *New York Times* proudly announced, "Physicists Finally Get to See Quantum Jump With Own Eyes" when for the first time in history, scientists were able to see something that had been theoretically envisioned for decades, but was thought to be outside the realm of human sensory experience. For decades, physicists had been working under the assumption that quantum jumps were happening, despite never once having actually witnessed such a jump.

Dr. Warren Nagourney of the University of Washington described the palpable excitement felt by the teams of physicists who first witnessed quantum particles making quantum jumps,

> *"You have to hold yourself steady and look for minutes at a time, and then you'll see it switch. You see the trapped ion blinking on and off, and each blink is a quantum jump. It's a striking illustration that things occur discontinuously in nature."*

Columbia physicist I.I. Rabi, one of the original contributors to the theory sums up how it feels to witness quantum weirdness first-hand,

> *"The atom is in one state and moves to another, and you can't picture what it is in between, so you call this a quantum jump. In quantum mechanics, you don't ask what's the intermediate state because there ain't no intermediate state. It passes from one to the other in God's mysterious way."*

In many ways, quantum physics is the epitome of inscrutability. From the enigmatic way single quantum particles exhibit signs of acting like waves of energy that interfere with unseen, unobserved other "particles" behaving like waves, to the mysterious ways quantum particles move in perfect instantaneous synchronization across great distances... there is something essentially incomprehensible and mysterious about quantum mechanics.

In March 2010, Aaron O'Connell and fellow physics researchers at UC Santa Barbara presented thrilling evidence of having witnessed visible evidence of a tiny strip of resonating metal existing in a superimposed state. The strip of metal was both vibrating and not vibrating at the same time, thanks to it being connected to a superconducting qubit—a very special solid state electrical circuit composed of inductors, capacitors, and Josephson junctions. The superconducting qubit acts like a bridge between the microscopic and macroscopic worlds. "It's like you have a child's swing that goes back and forth. We pushed the swing and didn't push the swing at the same time," said O'Connell. And like the proverbial "watched pot," this superposition of pushed-swing and not-pushed-swing only existed when not observed. While we haven't yet demonstrated full macroscopic scale quantum superposition of states, physicists anticipate such things will likely be possible in the next twenty years.

The notion that at its very foundation, nature is discontinuous with superimposed possible reality states simultaneously co-existing might at first seem to run completely counter to our common assumptions about reality. We commonly assume that reality functions as it appears to operate at our human scale of interaction, based on observing ordinary objects in our everyday world. Since we typically don't witness objects disappearing one moment and reappearing a moment later, blipping into and out of existence, the notion of such discrete now-you-see-it, now-you-don't types of events would seem supernatural should we witness such things in ordinary daily life.

When we consider that all matter, including ourselves, is involved in doing these blips into and out of physical form, and that according to known physical theories, such macroscopic larger-scale jumps are entirely possible, the multiverse we live in starts to feel much more magically, vibrantly alive.

What are Quantum Jumps?

The popular expression "quantum jump" is used in common English speech to describe a leap that is big—but to physicists, quantum jumps are tiny, discrete (indivisible), and abrupt. The idea of quantum particles is that they can exist in material form at one energy level or another, but not in between. When quantum particles are observed to make a quantum jump from one state to another, scientists watch them appear to blink on and off.

Quantum jumping is the process by which a person envisions some desired result or state of being that is different from the existing situation—and by clearly observing that possibility and supplying sufficient energy, makes a leap into that alternate reality. The idea behind quantum jumping is that we are living in a multiverse of parallel universes. Usually, these alternate realities have no connection to one another. A quantum jump can be made through a kind of handshake through time and space—this connection forms a bridge that allows someone experiencing a quantum jump to physically end up in another reality. The connection is so total that a person can literally walk into another place and time. While to the universe, both of "you" still exists, your awareness of who you are coalesces in one reality, often leaving the other out of reach, out of sight, and out of mind.

Does any of this seem outlandish or too far-out to be real? While quantum jumping may at first sound like an idea from science fiction, this term actually covers a wide range of experiences from the rather mundane to the truly extraordinary.

As you learn more about various examples of quantum jumps, you'll likely recognize common experiences from your daily life when you've made quantum jumps—often without realizing it at the time.

Imagine the example of a child who receives a mother's kiss after falling down and skinning a knee who suddenly feels much better... or any of a number of clinical trial participants with headaches who, upon taking a placebo (such as a sugar pill), is amazed to find a terrible headache suddenly gone. Visualize another example of a man preparing for an interview by dressing for success, in attire worn by those making the hiring decisions. In these examples, we find no material-based reason for why the child and clinical study participant are feeling much better and the interviewee feeling so much more confident and self-assured, but chances are very good that we've felt such inexplicably dramatic improvements many times in our lives over the years.

Some quantum jumps can literally be leaps to a better future, as seen in the real-life example of Ashley Clouse's ten feet leap to safety in the face of an oncoming tornado. We are capable of taking hundreds of quantum leaps in any given day, making decisions that seem inconsequential or small at the time, yet that have the collective power to entirely transform our lives. A daily decision to spend a few minutes writing, exercising, or practicing music makes a tremendous difference in a person's life over a period of weeks, months, and years.

In most cases, people experience walking into parallel worlds that are nearly—but not quite entirely—identical to the one they came from. In such cases, it is possible to find something has seemingly shifted in some startling way. A door or building may appear where one had not been before, or you might notice your keys are not where you left them ... and after searching for a while, be surprised to find them in a very odd place or a place you'd already searched with no apparent explanation. These types of reality shifts are remarkably commonplace, yet unless we pay attention to them, they often go unnoticed and unannounced.

How are Quantum Jumps Possible?

Consider the idea that many times—possibly even every time—you make a decision or choice, you are actually moving between alternate realities—between parallel worlds. In those alternate realities there is another possible "you" who you can connect with so strongly that the conscious awareness and energy that is you literally moves into that other reality. When feeling so strongly connected to another self in a different reality, it is possible to gain direct access to the knowledge available only in that time and space, and to experience an entirely different self.

What makes quantum jumping possible is that, like a quantum particle, every person has the ability to exhibit quantum behavior. While it may seem extremely improbable that you can do the things quantum particles do—such as tunnel through solid barriers, or make quantum jumps to other alternate times and places—our current understanding of physics suggests such things are within the realm of possibility, and can be expected to occur.

Experimental observations at the quantum level change our assumptions about reality as we see that: quantum particles are not always particles and sometimes exist as pure energy; some kind of invisible connection exists between entangled quantum particles so they move together simultaneously with non-local spooky action at a distance; simply by observing an experiment we are affecting it; and unlike classical physics, quantum behavior can only ever be predicted by probabilities.

In order to explain some of this truly strange quantum behavior, Niels Bohr theorized that quantum particles exist as waves that might be anywhere until the wave function is collapsed. Hugh Everett III theorized that we exist in an multiverse consisting of many worlds of parallel realities. Physicist John Cramer theorizes it is possible for information to be exchanged between past and future through a kind of handshake between two points in spacetime. Scientists David Bohm and Karl Pribram proposed the universe is a giant hologram, containing matter and consciousness in a single field.

What all this means to someone experiencing a quantum jump is that they can enter another parallel reality by relaxing and imagining they are accessing some kind of bridge, window, or doorway to another world with another self who has another set of characteristics, qualities, or skills. With quantum jumping, one makes the leap from simply *imagining* oneself in an alternate reality to actually *being* that other self. In this fashion, a mother who'd moments earlier stood atop a huge boulder holding her child's hand as an enormous tornado raced their way can switch from not being able to imagine herself jumping straight down off a boulder to making that ten foot leap to safety.

The success of most all visualization methods, affirmations, faking it 'til you make it, the placebo effect, and even simply getting out of bed when you don't feel like it can be attributed to quantum jumping.

Quantum Jumps Example: Getting Out of Bed

The idea of noticing a state of mind change that happens in an instant is described by American psychologist William James when considering the subject of will,

"We know what it is to get out of bed on a freezing morning in a room without a fire, and how the very vital principle within us protests against the ordeal. Probably most persons have lain on certain mornings for an hour at a time unable to brace themselves to the resolve. We think how late we shall be, how the duties of the day will suffer; we say, 'I must get up, this is ignominious,' etc.; but still the warm couch feels too delicious, the cold outside too cruel, and resolution faints away and postpones itself again and again just as it seemed on the verge of bursting the resistance and passing over into the decisive act. Now how do we ever get up under such circumstances? If I may generalize from my own experience, we more often than not get up without any struggle or decision at all. We suddenly find that we have got up. A fortunate lapse of consciousness occurs; we forget both the warmth and the cold; we fall into some revery connected with the day's life, in the course of which the idea flashes across us, 'Hollo! I must lie here no longer'—an idea which at that lucky instant awakens no contradictory or paralyzing suggestions, and consequently produces immediately its appropriate motor effects. It was our acute consciousness of both the warmth and the cold during the period of struggle, which paralyzed our activity then and kept our idea of rising in the condition of wish and not of will. The moment these inhibitory ideas ceased, the original idea exerted its effects."

We often make these kinds of quantum jumps through switching from one intention: *I'll just lie here in bed a little while longer*—to another: *It's time for me to get up and get going* —without giving much thought to the amazing quantum jump we've just achieved within ourselves.

Placebos and Quantum Jumps

For most of us, our first encounter with placebos happened when we were children and had a skinned knee, cut, or other "boo-boo" that we told our Mom or Dad about. Every child who asks, "Mommy, kiss it better," expects and receives one of the most powerful components of placebo or "sham" medical treatments.

Do you remember a time when getting over a cold, when all of a sudden you *knew* you were getting better? It's almost like a switch was flipped from "sick" to "well," and even though you might still have had the occasional sniffle or cough, you knew you were not sick anymore. The transition of going from sick to not-sick can happen amazingly fast. Such instantaneous wellness is a natural process, as we move from one state to another, and it's a perfect example of quantum jumping from one reality to another.

What if these "sham" treatments actually work? Our bias against placebos may primarily be due to our own historical inability to correctly attribute a legitimate healing mechanism to a genuinely powerful healing therapy. Quantum jumping can provide us with a mechanism by which placebo treatments of all types take effect in harmonious accordance with the body's natural healing abilities.

It's a well-known fact within the pharmaceutical industry that new drugs compete not just against one another, but also against the mighty placebo. A surprisingly large percentage of patients report feeling markedly better after taking a "sugar pill" or some other similar type of treatment with no known benefit. If simply by taking a sugar pill we set in motion a quantum jump, the placebo effect takes on entirely new significance. If all that is needed is permission for a patient to switch gears from one reality of illness to make a jump to another reality of improved health, quantum jumping might just be one of the best "new" treatments around.

Some clinical drug trials have proven quite embarrassing, thanks to unanticipated placebo effects, such as Genentech's trial for VEGF, a genetically engineered heart drug. Two months after treatments, patients who received low doses of VEGF could walk 26 seconds longer on a treadmill, those who received high doses could walk 32 seconds longer, and those who received just the placebo could walk the longest—42 seconds longer!

If placebos are so powerful, what have we learned so far about how they work? Serious investigation into what makes placebos tick has only recently begun. The newly-founded Harvard-affiliated Program in Placebo Studies and the Therapeutic Encounter (PiPS) based at Beth Israel Deaconess Medical Center in Boston, Massachusetts is the first multidisciplinary institute dedicated entirely to studying *how* the placebo effect works. Preliminary findings indicate a connection between the most successful placebo treatments and endorphins... yet endorphins in and of themselves don't fully explain all the tremendous positive results placebos achieve. As Harvard Associate Professor of Medicine Ted Kaptchuk discovered when running experiments to sort out the various components of placebo treatment, the *methods* of placebo administration are every bit as important as the administration itself.

Even Deception-Free Placebos Are Powerfully Effective

During past decades when no mechanism to account for the placebo effect was officially recognized, patients were seldom pleased to learn they were assigned to be members of placebo groups. Even the word placebo has a slight stigma to it, with its

Latin translation meaning, "I shall please," and having a history from the Middle Ages of referring to professional mourners-for-hire who sang at funeral masses, pretending to be the sorrowful bereaved.

Perhaps thanks to increasing awareness of the power of the placebo effect, there are increasing numbers of cases in which experimental subjects who were told they were receiving the placebo significantly improved! It does seem to help when study administrators include in their presentation along the lines of, "Do you know what a sugar pill is? A sugar pill is a pill with no medicine in it at all. I think this pill will help you as it has helped so many others. Are you willing to try this pill?" The previous statement was part of a standardized script, which was read to participants in a now classic non-blind placebo study from 1965.

Part of what makes this small-scale study so fascinating is that all fourteen participants experienced marked improvement after a one week trial. As doctors Lee Park and Uno Covi state in the summary of their paper, *"...patients can be willing to take placebo and can improve despite disclosure of the inert content of the pills; belief in pill as drug was not a requirement for improvement."*

Placebos Are Getting Stronger

Along with the surprising fact that the placebo effect is strong amongst dogs and other animals is that the placebo effect is getting increasingly stronger in humans over time. Arthur Barsky, director of psychiatric research at Brigham and Women's Hospital in Boston, says:

> *"The placebo response was about twice as powerful than it was in the 1980s."*

When asked why these placebos work so well when there's no material reason they should, Barsky explains it's a matter of conditioning. Just the fact that you are involved in a pattern of behavior you associate with healing increases the odds you'll be successfully healed.

Placebos Work for Animals

Dogs given placebos in double-blind studies for epilepsy-related medication benefited positively, as did dogs suffering from osteoarthritis. When 58 arthritic dogs were assessed for lameness by owners and veterinarians in a randomized double-blind FDA-approved trial, owners of dogs given the placebo non-steroidal anti-inflammatory medication reported improvement in their dogs mobility 56.9% of the time, with veterinarians reporting between 40% and 45% improvement in dogs given placebos. Even though this study was designed to determine to what degree pet owners see subjective improvement compared the objective veterinarian platform gait analysis for dogs, it found a phenomenally large unbiased measurable placebo effect both in reduction of lameness at a trot, and reduction of pain on palpation of the joints.

There appears to be a great deal more to the external factors associated with healing than has historically been fully considered, with animals, humans, and perhaps even plants benefiting from tender loving care.

Placebos and Nocebos

Yet another fascinating aspect of placebos is that not only do placebos provide relief, but they often do so in the same pattern one would expect if the patients had been taking the actual treatment, as psychiatrist Dr. Walter A. Brown of Brown University describes,

> *"... this is very telling, I think — when placebos are given for pain management, the course of pain relief follows what you would get with an active drug. The peak relief comes about an hour after it's administered, as it does with the real drug, and so on. If placebo analgesia was the equivalent of giving nothing, you'd expect a more random pattern."*

Patients who expect a given treatment to have a certain result will tend to experience that result, including in many cases, expected side-effects. Such side-effects are known as the 'nocebo.' The Latin meaning for the term 'nocebo' reaction chosen by Walter Kennedy is "I shall harm." Mr. Kennedy noted that there was an evident need to talk about the way some study participants were surprisingly adversely affected by something as seemingly innocuous as sugar pills.

Research study results indicate that when people are warned of possible pain or side effects, such warnings increase the likelihood that they'll experience those problems in a nocebo reaction. Conversely, when people are reassured that many people benefit from the sham treatment, they often do improve, even when told what they are taking is a placebo. Research studies on the nocebo effect tend to be rare, due to ethical problems of how to conduct studies that yield valid results without deceiving study participants and inducing needless pain and suffering.

Some scientists, including physician-bioethicist Howard Brody, were skeptical that the nocebo effect was real... until Italian neurophysiologist Fabrizio Benedetti at the University of Turin Medical School conducted a study that clearly indicated a neural mechanism driving the body's nocebo response.

Postoperative patients in Benedetti's study were given either a saline solution or proglumide. While neither injection actually caused any discomfort, patients receiving saline injections experienced increased pain. When patients received proglumide, they had no increase in pain (no nocebo effect). Benedetti discovered that the hypothalamic-pituitary-adrenal axis in the brain, an important part of the body's 'stress system,' is activated during a nocebo response, as shown by an increase in the secretion of the hormones associated with anxiety: ACTH from the pituitary gland, and cortisol from the adrenal gland.

Despite growing interest in the nocebo effect, ethical and legal concerns have nearly slowed research to a standstill. "My ethics committee will not allow me to do it," says psychologist Paul Ench of the University of Tübingen in Germany... unless he agrees to inform experimental subjects he is deceiving them.

Thanks to research into the nocebo effect, the conflict between 'informed consent' and 'first, do no harm' becomes clear. Detailed medical consent forms have been shown to contribute to stated yet seldom-anticipated side-effects. One way to minimize nocebo effects is for medical caregivers to consistently word all treatment-related conversations positively, rather than negatively, giving percentages of people who benefit from procedures, and percentages of people who are pain-free afterward with no side effects.

Such a positive focus could help reduce and eliminate cases such as the one that recently occurred when a patient participating in a trial for antidepressant medication consumed twenty-six placebo pills in a suicide attempt. Even though the placebo pills had no active ingredients, his blood pressure plummeted to dangerously low levels.

Quantum Jumps Example: Pharmaceutical Placebo

A recently published study stated that most family doctors have given one or more of their patients a placebo drug. 97% of 783 general practitioners admitted to having prescribed sugar pills or some other type of treatment with no established efficacy.

Far from initiating a scandal, this news may actually do a great deal of good. Doctors and the general public are becoming increasingly aware that the placebo's effect's track record is truly impressive, and therefore may be condoned as preferable to taking no action at all. Very few legitimate pharmaceutical prescriptions can match, let alone exceed the absolutely astonishing placebo track record for success, with some 35% to 75% of placebo recipients with ailments ranging from arthritis to depression reporting substantial and in some cases lasting improvement.

Quantum Jumps Example: Faith Aids Therapy

When researchers at McLean Hospital in Belmont, Massachusetts set out to study psychiatric treatment effectiveness in 159 men and women suffering from depression, anxiety, and bipolar disorder, they asked study participants one question: "To what extent do you believe in God?"

Randi McCabe, director of the Anxiety Treatment and Research Center at St. Joseph's Healthcare in Ontario commented,

> *"Your belief that you're going to get better, your attitude, does influence how you feel. And really, in cognitive behavior therapy, that is really what we're trying to change: peoples' beliefs, how they're seeing their world, their perspective."*

While the strength of peoples' beliefs was unrelated to their initial symptoms when admitted for treatment, it turned out to be surprisingly indicative of the efficacy of therapy. As David H. Rosmarin, the study's lead author reports,

"Patients who had higher levels of belief in God demonstrated more effects of treatment. They seemed to get more bang for their buck, so to speak."

Quantum Jumps Example: Surgical Placebo

In summer 1994, surgeon J. Bruce Moseley was engaged in an elaborately arranged small-scale pilot study with ten middle-aged former military men. These ten volunteers knew they would be randomly assigned to one of three different groups: standard arthroscopic surgery (scraping and rinsing of the knee joints), rinsing of the knee joints with no scraping, and "sham" or placebo surgery with pretend surgery. Dr. Moseley would stab the placebo patients' knees three times with a scalpel in a way that would create incisions and scars later on, but his behavior before, during, and after all three types of operations was to be the same. This was made somewhat easier by the fact that he'd only find out moments before the actual operation which type of procedure he'd be performing. Bruce Moseley, team physician for the Houston Rockets, started out with no expectation for positive results from the placebo surgery group; he was participating in the study in the first place because he was skeptical about the benefit of arthroscopic surgery to treat arthritis. Dr. Nelda Wray was in charge of health research at the Houston V.A., and asked Moseley how he could tell if those who improved from surgery weren't benefiting primarily due to the placebo effect. Moseley was stunned by this question and responded, "It can't be. This is surgery we're talking about." Dr. Wray replied,

"You're all wrong. The bigger and more dramatic the patient perceives the intervention to be, the bigger the placebo effect. Big pills have more than small pills, injections have more than pills and surgery has the most of all."

In this first small-scale study, the placebo worked like a charm. Even six months post operation, none of the patients knew which group they were in, and all ten men reported greatly reduced pain. The study was repeated, this time with 180 patients, and with similar results.

Many people were surprised to discover the astonishing efficacy of placebo surgeries, in such studies as the ones reported in the New England Journal of Medicine involving arthroscopic knee surgery in 2002 and 2008. Positive improvements have been seen in 50% of study participants receiving placebo surgery for Parkinson's disease, with most positive results associated with the most invasive placebo surgeries, and the most advanced cases of Parkinson's disease.

Numerous additional surgical studies have shown phenomenal powers of placebo medical treatments for everything ranging from painting warts with brightly colored inert dye (with warts falling off when the color wore off); to doctors telling asthmatics they were inhaling a bronchiodilator when they weren't; to fake ultrasound for post wisdom-tooth extraction patients relieving pain; to incisions made in peoples' chests by Seattle cardiologist Leonard Cobb, as sham variations of the then-popular internal mammary ligation surgery resulting in increased blood flow to the heart.

With such consistently positive results from placebo surgeries and medical treatments, it's clear there must be a reason for all this success—and quantum jumping can help explain these wonderful results.

Quantum Jumps Example: Academic Placebo

If you've suffered from test anxiety, or wished there was an easier way to get a boost when taking tests—there's some really good news from an unexpected source. Placebos turn out to not just be useful for medical treatments—they are also proving effective for helping students perform better on multiple choice tests. German psychologist Ulrich Weger and Australian psychologist Stephen Loughnan devised an experiment by which 40 undergraduate students were given a 20 question general knowledge test, with each question having four possible answers.

Subjects were informed that before each question was asked, the correct answer would be momentarily flashed upon the screen too quickly for them to consciously recognize, but they were assured that the correct answer would register subconsciously in their brains. In actuality, what was being flashed momentarily had nothing at all to do with the correct answers, but was instead a bit of gibberish consisting of random strings of letters.

Weger and Loughnan found that participants who believed they'd subliminally received the correct answers flashed quickly on the screen and given verbal guidance by experimenters, *"On some level, you already know the answer,"* scored significantly higher than participants in the control group who received no similar verbal guidance nor subliminal gibberish flashing on their computer screens.

The researchers conclude that when you're confident, *"anxieties that have previously taxed cognitive resources... become available for other tasks and processes."* Clearly the best possible mantra or affirmation to tell oneself before taking any test is, *"you know this."*

Quantum Jumps Example: Visualize Steps to Success

Some of the most effective weight loss programs help people lose pounds by imagining they now live in an alternate reality in which they are already thin. What's especially interesting is that recent research indicates that *how* we do our visualization makes a difference. A study by psychologists Lien B. Pham and Shelley E. Taylor compared the effectiveness of visualizing the process versus the outcome, and their finding showed that *visualizing the process* is significantly more effective. In other words, those who pictured themselves making healthier choices such as choosing to eat fresh vegetables instead of junk food, rather than just imagining themselves to be skinnier, had an easier time actually choosing celery and hummus, for example, over ice cream as a snack.

Many top athletes use visualization of perfect performance together with envisioning they can become that top athlete to improve their athletic results in real life. Once again, it really helps to envision oneself engaged in perfect practice—not just winning first place in a competition.

Quantum Jumps Example: Fake It 'til You Make It

When someone says "I'm faking it 'til I make it," they might well be visualizing themselves as being an entirely transformed person. A person who wants a promotion can thus emulate the dress, speech, behavior, self assurance and posture of someone at the next level up, to be considered *deserving* of a promotion.

Some of the requisite "how to" steps to visualize are surprisingly easy, such as simply donning the appropriate attire. A recent study at the Kellogg School of Management at Northwestern University reports that when research subjects wore a white coat and were told it was a scientist's or medical doctor's white coat, they performed better on a cognitive test known as the "Stroop test," where they are asked to say the color of a word being shown rather than the word itself, making half as many errors as their control group peers. Intriguingly, those who donned white jackets and were told they were artist's coats did not perform above average, which would seem to indicate that people's interpretations of the symbolic meaning of clothing can make a difference in peoples' cognitive abilities.

Why Do Quantum Jumps Occur?

In order to understand quantum jumps, it's essential that we fully appreciate what "quantum" means. The word "quantum" in the field of physics is defined in the Oxford dictionary as being:

"a discrete quantity of energy proportional in magnitude to the frequency of the radiation it represents."

and "quantum mechanics" is defined as:

"the branch of mechanics that deals with the mathematical description of the motion and interaction of subatomic particles, incorporating the concepts of quantization of energy, wave-particle duality, the uncertainty principle, and the correspondence principle."

The whole reason this field of physics studying the very small sprang up in the first place was in pursuit of the true nature of reality. *"What is the true nature of reality?"* has been the guiding question inspiring generations of physicists to pursue ever smaller particles on the quest to find the most fundamental irreducible 'building block' from which all that we see and know to be real springs forth. Atoms were found to consist of protons, neutrons and electrons—spinning so rapidly through mostly wide open spaces while invisible to the human eye—yet we know they exist, thanks to experiments with "atom-smashers." Early discoveries of even smaller bits of matter rocked the world in the 20th century. But the most unsettling thing to scientists wasn't so much the miniscule size of these quantum particles as it was the way these quantum particles behave.

Quantum Weirdness on the Macro Scale

There are many types of behaviors exhibited at the quantum level that we don't expect to see on the 'macro scale' of our daily lives, mostly because we're unaware of being readily able to observe them with our ordinary senses. Our perception of our world in this new Quantum Age is about to undergo something on par with the Copernican Revolution. In the Copernican Revolution of the 16th century, most people worldwide changed their mental model of our solar system from envisioning the sun and planets revolving around the Earth to realizing the Earth revolves around the sun. This changing worldview depends on scientific observations of quantum behavior on the macroscopic scale of physical objects we can readily observe with our ordinary senses. Such aspects of quantum weirdness include: quantum superposition of states, quantum coherence, quantum entanglement, quantum tunneling, and quantum teleportation:

Quantum Superposition of States

Quantum superposition is a fundamental principle in quantum mechanics by which all possibilities for something in material form exist simultaneously in all possible particular states (or all possible configurations of its properties)—but whenever measured or observed, the result corresponds to only one of those possible states or configurations.

Quantum Coherence

Quantum coherence is another basic principle in quantum mechanics by which in any given quantum system, all parts of that system remain in perfect synchronization with one another. There is currently no observable mechanism by which a given quantum system achieves such a state, yet this feature of coherence allows quantum systems to achieve amazing levels of efficiency.

Quantum Entanglement

Physicist Erwin Schrödinger introduced entanglement as a correlation of different measurement outcomes with the German word 'Verschränkung', stating, "Maximal knowledge of a whole system does not necessarily include knowledge of all of its parts, even if these are totally divided from each other and do not influence each other at the present time." There is a level of interconnectedness by which quantum particles move in simultaneous synchronization, even when separated by distance in space.

Quantum Tunneling

Quantum tunneling is a quantum mechanical effect in which particles have a finite probability of crossing an energy barrier, such as the energy needed to break a bond with another particle, even when that quantum particle's energy is less than the energy barrier. Because matter is both particle and waves, something can exist on one side of a barrier, then exist in energy wave form, and then be observed on the other side of a barrier.

Quantum Teleportation

Quantum teleportation is a term used to describe the instantaneous transference of properties from one quantum system to another without physical contact.

As for what *causes* such remarkable behavior at the quantum level of reality—nobody really knows for sure. The mathematical equations describing quantum behavior work beautifully well, yet the behind-the-scenes why and how of it are anything but obvious. There are numerous physics theories that each explain what's going on in their own unique ways, and these theories are known as 'interpretations' since they provide us with possible explanations for what might be going on, based on sound assumptions. Chief among these theories which seem to do an excellent job of accounting for "quantum weirdness" are: John Cramer's Transactional Interpretation, Hugh Everett III's Many Worlds Interpretation (MWI), David Bohm's Holographic Interpretation, Leonard Susskind and Raphael Bousso's Holographic Multiverse Interpretation, and Niels Bohr's Copenhagen Interpretation.

John Cramer's Transactional Interpretation

—'handshake' between future and past

John Cramer's transactional interpretation of quantum physics suggests that "handshakes" take place between quantum particles in different points in time and space. In Cramer's interpretation, a particle here and now on Earth instantaneously communicates with particles light-years away in time and space, as one particle sends an "offer" wave and another responds with a "confirmation" wave.

Hugh Everett III's Many Worlds Interpretation (MWI)

—many parallel worlds

In the 1950's, Hugh Everett III proposed that every possibility inherent in each wave function is real, and that ALL of them occur. Possibilities become actualities with each measurement that is made, and infinite slightly different realities come into existence as each quantum event is observed. All possibilities are equally real in the multiverse. Parallel universes coexist side-by-side, undetected by one another.

David Bohm's Holographic Interpretation

—enfolded order

University of London physicist David Bohm and Stanford University neurophysiologist Karl Pribram proposed that the universe may be like a giant hologram, containing both matter and consciousness as a single field. This model suggests that the objective world "out there" is a vast ocean of waves and frequencies which appears solid to us because our brains convert that enfolded hologram into unfolded physical material we can perceive with our senses. As the English poet William Blake explains, we thus *"... see a world in a grain of sand."*

Niels Bohr's Copenhagen Interpretation

—popping the 'qwif' / collapsing the wave function

The Copenhagen Interpretation of quantum physics was first described and presented by Niels Bohr in Italy in 1927. Bohr suggested that quantum particles exist as waves which might be anywhere until the wave function is collapsed. As long as nobody looks, each quantum particle is equally distributed in a series of overlapping probability waves, in a superposition of states. An observer is required to assist in ensuring quantum choices are made.

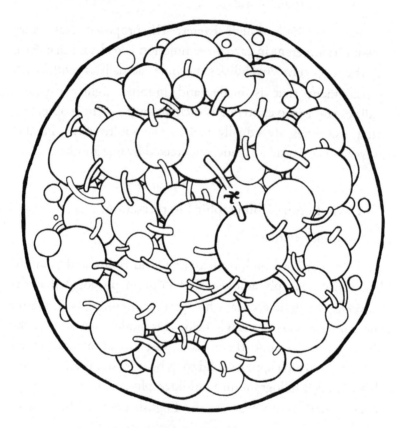

Holographic Multiverse Interpretation

—many unified parallel worlds

UC Berkeley's physicists Leonard Susskind and Raphael Bousso assert that the global multiverse is a representation of the many worlds, within a single holographic superstructure providing enclosed universes with boundaries. All the physics of the multiverse is encoded upon the boundary in time of the surrounding superstructure, where time is set to infinity. Observers are aware of their own slices of reality in space and time within their respective universes.

Interpreting Quantum Jumps

It's important to note that all the above possible explanations for what's happening on the quantum level end with the word "interpretation," reminding us that no physicist yet lays claim to anything akin to a quantum "law" of physics. The best that's so far been achieved are some beautiful possible topographies, and elegant mathematical descriptions. It is clear that John Cramer's Transactional Interpretation of quantum mechanics offers some uniquely helpful insights to assist anyone desiring a quantum jump, as does the relatively new Holographic Multiverse Interpretation. I love the idea that quantum theories can be combined to create imaginative new interpretations, in much the same way that chefs create exotically delicious concoctions such as Thai-flavored Mexican burritos!

It's entirely possible that rather than just one of the above interpretations being correct and all others incorrect, several theories may be working together. The Holographic Multiverse Interpretation, for example, is a combination of the Holographic Interpretation with the Many Worlds Interpretation that provides a more holistic, integrated version of many possible worlds. Within a holographic multiverse, there is an interconnectedness between each part of any given parallel universe and all other possible parallel worlds within that holographic multiverse. When the Holographic Multiverse Interpretation is combined with the Transactional Interpretation, we gain an extraordinary view of reality that can truly broaden our minds.

The Transactional Interpretation involves absorption and emission of waves, with perfect symmetry occurring between emitted and absorbed waves. In essence, what is happening is a synchronized behind-the-scenes choreography in which one point in spacetime communicates with another in something akin to a handshake. When you realize that some information is moving forward in time and some backwards through time, there is equal significance to receiving information as there is to sending it—both are equally active and involved. As physicist Ruth Kastner points out,

> *"Why should Nature care whether we 'observe' or not ...?*
> *The only way that Nature could know or care would be*
> *because something physical really happens in such*
> *'observations,' and the only possible physical process*
> *accompanying an 'observation' is absorption."*

Evidence of Transactional Interpretation & Bicausality

Those of us who've ever experienced precognition, premonitions, intuitive hunches, synchronicity, and déjà vu have received experiential first-hand personal evidence of other possibilities that we can vote on with our emotional reactions. As soon as we have any kind of emotional reactions, our emotions can assist us in flipping between coherent, coupled realities. An example of such a flip-flop is deciding at last that it really IS time to get out of bed, but then feeling it would be lovely to enjoy the peaceful tranquility of relaxing comfortably in bed for a few moments more.

While these types of experiences can be extraordinary and deeply meaningful when they occur, their very nature does not render them suitable for laboratory experimentation. Even though reproducible experiments in these areas may be harder to come by, they can still be studied in much the same way naturalists observe wild plants, animals and ecosystems: utilizing powers of observation, and detailed note-taking.

Some studies have consistently shown a seeming reversal between cause and effect, much as we'd expect to see from time-to-time in a universe according to the Transactional Interpretation. Such reverse-direction causality is sometimes referred to as retrocausality, while the term bicausality refers to inclusion of both forward and backward through time causality. Studies conducted at Princeton Engineering Anomalies Research (PEAR) by researchers Robert Jahn and Brenda Dunne, for example, showed experimental subjects could influence coin flips equally well either before or after the coins were actually flipped. In 2001, Leonard Leibovici published results from his double-blind study of more than three thousand patients that demonstrated that people who had been prayed for some four to ten years later experienced considerably shorter hospital stays and shorter periods of fever.

Scientific evidence of retrocausality includes a 2008 study by University of Illinois physicists Onur Hosten and Paul Kwiat, who detected a shift in a beam of polarized light moving between air and glass that was influenced by a *future* decision.

In 2009, American physicist John Howell of the University of Rochester reported success in using weak, less obtrusive, measurements to show that light traveling along the observed gate was amplified by a factor of more than 100 when influenced by a *future choice* in the experiment.

Advantages in viewing the universe through Transactional Interpretation "handshake-between-past-and-future" lenses includes that those of us who are aware of experiencing things like premonitions and déjà vu have a scientific mechanism to account for what's going on. Not only does the Transactional Interpretation model provide us with a context by which we move through many possible realities, but it allows for forward-through-time and backward-through-time communication to occur.

How Do Quantum Jumps Work?

You've probably heard of self-fulfilling prophecies in which people often experience that which they expect. Professional athletes take advantage of this phenomenon by practicing visualization of perfect performance, in order to get the best results.

Starting with an understanding that everything is made up of quantum material at its very core, the idea behind quantum jumps is that it's possible to jump to an alternate reality in much the same way that an electron dematerializes at one orbital level and reappears at another. The fundamental principles behind quantum jumping are based upon the behavior of these very smallest particles known in physics—quantum particles. There is a superposition of states in the time of dematerialization in which a quantum particle is between states, and is behaving like pure energy rather than like a particular piece of matter. Just as electrons can make energetic leaps from one energetic level to another, people can quantum jump through alternate realities to experience dramatic shifts in physical reality. Quantum jumps can be envisioned as occurring in a multiverse of many alternate realities. Within each one of these realities exists another possible 'you' that you can just as easily be.

Anyone who can relax, clear their mind, and envision being different in some way—such as more successful, funny, healthy, wealthy, or wise—can quantum jump. To initiate a quantum jump requires keeping an open mind that you can experience another reality. It is important that you are able to sincerely desire and feel a connection to another reality, envisioning some way of making a connection with it through a bridge, a door, a window or a handshake.

Your ability to form a strong intention, to concentrate, and to get and stay focused while feeling detached from concerns of daily life—relaxed, open-minded, and emotionally energized—are essential. Just as when you shift gears on your car, you must first disengage from one gear before re-engaging in a new gear, you must attain a mindset of detachment in order to release connections to physical realities you have felt locked into with your thoughts and feelings. Detachment and disengagement gives you a necessary break from identifying as who you've thought you are, so you can experience the ecstasy of feeling relaxed and energized in a state of pure consciousness for a little while. In such a state of pure consciousness, you become aware that you are capable of sensing all possible realities, and you realize that you can emerge from this meditation or lucid dream into the best possible reality for you.

* * *

The next chapter, *Why Do We Quantum Jump?* examines that very question from two different yet complementary perspectives. Chapter Two explores both the reasons that quantum jumping is physically possible in the first place, and also common reasons people have for enjoying experiencing quantum jumps in their lives.

Exercise

Imagine Many Possible You's

Close your eyes and imagine the possibility that at every decision point in your life so far, there are other possible you's living out every single other path you could have taken. Visualize how many of those other possible you's have gained tremendous strength, courage, confidence, wealth, happiness and health. Imagine that you can live a happier, more prosperous life by making a leap into the realities in which you have those qualities you'd most like to have, and that each time you make a choice and take action, you're making a quantum jump.

Exercise

Remember What You Desire

Think about something you truly desire. Notice how you feel in your body while thinking about it. Next, imagine the object of your desire is here right now, and has come through for you. Think of this scenario as being a memory, and notice how you feel (most likely happier and more upbeat). Any time you notice yourself wistfully wishing for what you desire, switch over to remembering it as a "done deal" once again— connecting with the possible reality in which it already exists.

Exercise

Imagine a Lamp Quantum Jump

Imagine what it would be like to gaze calmly at a desk lamp while it shines brightly and stays in one place... until suddenly, without any warning or fanfare, like a quantum particle making a leap... it's gone. Imagine that you see the desk lamp blink out of existence here... vanishing to who-knows-where... and reappearing in a slightly different spot a moment later.

Exercise

Imagine Excellent Health

Think of an aspect of your current mental, physical, or emotional health that seems less than optimal, and imagine that you can jump to a reality where your health and well-being is significantly improved. Know that just as patients who knowingly take "sham" placebo treatments, the simple fact that you are taking a moment to care for yourself and your health makes a tremendous positive difference for you now. Breathe in deeply and fully and close your eyes, imagining that the energy from this full, deep breath is all that is required to help you first imagine and then jump to a reality in which you feel in excellent health. Envision what you are doing in this new reality to help maintain your improved state of well-being, and promise yourself that when you open your eyes you will do things that are consistently in your best interests for optimal health and well-being.

Exercise

Visualize New Daily Activities

Think of one particular change you'd love to make in your life in which you will enjoy improvements in your health, wealth, relationships or work. Close your eyes and breathe deeply as you imagine a tremendously positive reality with wonderfully enjoyable outcomes. Envision some ways your daily activities in your new life are quite different from your daily activities now. Pay special attention to the activities in this new reality that help contribute to improvements in your health, wealth, relationships, and work... and picture how these new activities are becoming your normal everyday activities. Promise yourself that when you open your eyes, you will do things that are in your best interests to ensure you stay aligned with this newly emerging reality.

"I believe we will continue to find increasingly strong reasons to believe that some of the strange effects observable in the microscopic world exist not only in the exotic realms, but also in more intimate domain of human experience.

I also believe that the implications of all this for understanding psi are sufficiently remote from engrained ways of thinking that the first reaction will be confidence that it's wrong. The second will be horror that it might be right. The third will be boredom, because it's obvious."

— *Dean Radin*

Chapter 2

Why Do We

Quantum Jump?

Romanian-born actress Florina Petcu received high praise in the *The New Yorker*'s review of her work with Denzel Washington in Spike Lee's *Inside Man* as a "shameless, cigarette-waving, Albanian floozy." Even as Florine's acting was being recognized as some of the film's best, *"I saw myself becoming someone I didn't like."*

In that moment, Florina realized, *"I was not Florina, I was the actress."* Fortunately for Florina, she'd been staying physically fit with Muay Thai boxing, where she says,

> *"I had found such a support system in this world that I*
> *never had in acting. I remember when another boxer*
> *asked me to hang out and I immediately thought: What*
> *do you want? I wasn't conditioned to think that she would*
> *just want to be friends because in the acting world,*
> *everyone is for themselves."*

Through her circle of friends in Muay Thai boxing, Petcu learned about the Somaly Mam Foundation, an organization that empowers survivors of sex trafficking, and learned that dance therapy helps children who suffer from post-traumatic stress disorder (PTSD). As Petcu learned more about how she could make a positive difference, she discovered the City University of New York's strong psychology program, and enrolled as a double-major in sports psychology and creative movement and drama therapy. By the end of her senior year at CUNY, thirty-seven year old Petcu was one of three captains on CUNY's first-ever woman's soccer team.

Quantum jumps require both a flash of insight that a new reality is possible, and a burst of sufficient energy to make the leap. Those decisive instants when we feel simultaneously energized by knowledge of a better reality and inspired to act are launch points for quantum jumps.

What makes Florina's story such a wonderful example of quantum jumping is that rather than passively observing that her life was beginning to veer off-course, Florina pictured a new reality in which she could become someone she likes who is more true to the socially involved, cooperative, educated woman she feels she truly is. As soon as Florina felt inspired by envisioning this more enjoyable possible future, she immediately took steps to make it so.

Before we explore the many motivations we might have to make a quantum jump, which could conceivably range from surviving crises in times of emergency all the way to finding our calling or losing weight, let's take a look at why we can be more certain than ever that quantum phenomena is occurring in our daily lives... that we truly are quantum jumping to other realities that already exist. The idea of quantum mechanics is still relatively new, and now that humanity has had a bit more than a hundred years to mull it over, we're finally starting to realize we are living in a Quantum Age.

Dawn of the Quantum Age

We are tremendously fortunate to be alive during a pivotal time in history in which we see ever-increasing evidence of quantum behavior on the macroscopic (larger-than-quantum-particle) scale. Birds do it... by utilizing a quantum Zeno effect that helps them determine the direction of the Earth's magnetic field. Plants do it when they photosynthesize, utilizing quantum coherence across protein matrices. Humans do it with every breath we take, when we smell... and we make use of quantum tunneling to pick up even the faintest whiffs from as little as just one odiferous molecule. Schrödinger's cat has jumped out of the box, as quantum physics joins with other scientific disciplines to create a new spectrum of interdisciplinary sciences including quantum biology, quantum chemistry, and quantum astronomy.

Propelling humanity's rush forward into the Quantum Age is the race to develop quantum computers. Quantum computers are to their predecessors as laptop computers are to typewriters... symbolic of one small step in technology that represents a giant leap for mankind. With quantum computers expected to imminently break out of the "binary" system of computing, we're poised to enter a whole new world so big we can hardly comprehend it from this side. Quantum computers utilize "qubits" rather than bits, which can simultaneously express more than one value, introducing a level of computation optimization on a blisteringly fast scale. For example, a quantum computer with 300 qubits could run more calculations in an instant than there are atoms in the universe.

As in all previous transition points from Stone Age to Bronze Age, to Iron Age, to Agricultural Age, to Industrial Age to Information Age—the transition to Quantum Age will require us to adjust not only to using the newest tools of this new age, but also to incorporate the requisite thought patterns required to adapt to these new tools. As with all ages before it, the Quantum Age asks us how we plan to use its power, and what we are and aren't willing to give of ourselves in order to reap its benefits. And as with all previous ages, we will likely find ourselves immersed in the new quantum technology before we've properly considered how best to answer these questions, let alone what implications there are to how we choose to respond. We will benefit from considering potential opportunities and problems with the mindset of the Quantum Age by considering how this new era will affect our daily lives.

Now that we know that all manner of quantum weirdness and "spooky action at a distance" is part and parcel of the way our universe really works, we can no longer pretend that only the building blocks of matter exist in superimposed (multiple existence), entangled (non-local) states enjoying instantaneous communication with one another regardless of distance. At this juncture of crossing the threshold into the Quantum Age, two-thirds of physicists surveyed now believe that everything in material form—*including us*—exists in a superimposed state of many possible realities. The mind-boggling implication of this simple statement is that *there are many possible you's... and many possible me's.*

Not only are there many possible you's, but growing evidence—such as a dearth of other new particles found by the Large Hadron Collider in addition to the newly found Higgs boson—suggests that our universe is so statistically unlikely that it must be something of an aberration. The fact that we appear to live in such a statistically improbable universe is leading ever-increasing numbers of physicists to embrace Hugh Everett III's Many Worlds Interpretation (MWI) of quantum physics. The multiverse explanation for quantum mechanics got a big boost back in 1987, when Nobel Prize-winning physicist Steven Weinberg calculated that the cosmological constant of our universe—the energy density in otherwise empty space—is measured to be just as we would expect it according to the multiverse Many Worlds Interpretation.

How can the idea that there are many possible you's make a difference in your life? To begin with, envision that some of these possible you's have the secret to enjoying better health, relationships, career success, and fortune than you're currently experiencing. Possibly some of them are mastering new skills you've always wished you could learn, enjoying wonderful relationships, and exploring all kinds of creative hobbies and fascinating pursuits. Sound like fun? The good news is that with quantum jumping, it's easier than ever to make a leap into a life you love.

Even though a majority of physicists surveyed agreed we likely exist in a superimposed state, we are only just beginning to find direct physical evidence supporting theories of parallel universes. We are still waiting to see whether physicist Stephen Hawking's quest to find multiple sounds from many Big Bangs has anything to say about the matter, and physicists at an Italian university laboratory suspect their missing neutrons may be traveling to parallel worlds. Research scientists are discovering ever-increasing evidence of quantum behavior on the macroscopic (larger-than-quantum-particle) scale. At the same time as entangled diamonds and teleporting rubidium atoms bring quantum physics into the range of human sensing, a whole new frontier of quantum biology dawns. New studies show that the ability of plants to photosynthesize depends upon quantum superposition—as little packets of energy try all possible pathways until settling on the most efficient. Birds appear to navigate utilizing quantum entanglement, and our very human sense of smell appears to be dependent upon quantum tunneling, with electrons in the receptors of our noses disappearing on one side of an olfactory (smell) molecule, and reappearing on the other.

Seeking Evidence of Parallel Universes & Many Big Bangs

Physicists Stephen Hawking and Thomas Hertog called for the search for signs of multiple multiverse cosmic background radiation "Big Bangs," utilizing the concept of "Top-Down Cosmology," and the notion that our universe had more than one beginning and history. Thomas Hertog succinctly summarizes this big idea as,

"quantum physics forbids a single history."

The hunt is now on to see if more than one sound from many possible previous Big Bangs can be detected. Just as sound comes forth from erupting volcanos and exploding firecrackers, vibrations from the original Big Bang continue to ring through the universe. Hertog continues,

"Top down cosmology is testable, as it predicts variation in intensity of microwave background radiation from the Big Bang."

Finding Evidence of Many Worlds in Cosmic Radiation

In 2013, some of the first hard evidence of other universes was found through cosmic background radiation data collected by the European Space Agency's Planck telescope. Instruments aboard the Planck spacecraft took measurements of cosmic background radiation from the time of the Big Bang some 13.8 billion years ago, and scientists noted upon reviewing this data in the form of a cosmic gravity map that there was a surprising and significant concentration in the south half of the sky with a "cold spot" that could not easily be explained—other than as exactly the sort of anomalies predicted some eight years ago.

Theoretical physicist Laura Mersini-Houghton of the University of North Carolina at Chapel Hill and Carnegie Mellon professor Richard Holman were pleased to see that the very anomalies they predicted would be found when measuring background radiation have finally been observed. Dr. Mersini-Houghton explained, *"These anomalies were caused by other universes pulling on our universe as it formed during the Big Bang. They are the first hard evidence for the existence of other universes that we have seen."*

Mersini-Houghton and Holman's findings are especially exciting since they were predicted many years in advance, based on a quantum cosmology model of the multiverse, before they were physically confirmed by the Planck spacecraft measurements.

Vanishing Neutrons Provide Evidence of Parallel Worlds

In 2012, theoretical physicists from the University of l'Aquila, Italy found a mysterious anomaly; the loss rate of neutrons appeared to be dependent upon the strength and direction of a magnetic field. To say this finding was shocking is quite an understatement, since this strange behavior could not be explained by current theories of physics. Zurab Berezhiani proposed that perhaps the missing neutrons were visiting parallel universes. While researchers haven't yet conclusively proven this theory one way or the other, scientists have at the very least found something happening in nature that we would expect to see if parallel worlds really do exist.

Finding Evidence of Many Worlds in Alternate Histories

There is an exciting human side to the subject of alternate histories and parallel worlds. While we don't yet have technology to show photos from your past with evidence of parallel universes impinging on the very fabric of reality since the day you were born, we can look to see what kinds of evidence we are able to collect more easily. If we were feeling the effects of parallel universes, we would expect to occasionally notice that history doesn't stay put. Occasionally, we'd have very different ideas of what happened than we've had before, or than others have had before. What would such alternate histories be like?

Dr. Robert A. Burton recounts a fascinating experience in his book, *On Being Certain,* of attending a medical school reunion dinner in which conversation turned to where people were when they heard the news that Kennedy was assassinated. Burton and his classmates had all been in their second year of medical school, attending similar classes and hanging out together. An argument broke out amongst the reunion attendees as a urologist thought they were all at lunch, an internist remembered they'd been in the lab, and a pathologist remembered being at a pub down the street from the med center. With classmates turning to Burton to be the tie-breaker, setting history straight, the pathologist and urologist both agreed on one thing as they announced in unison, *"Everyone remembers the Kennedy assassination."*

If this was the first time such differences of memory related to significant events occurred, we might dismiss it as a humorous aside. But the fact of the matter is that researchers are increasingly becoming aware of what they call "false recollections." With the advent of the Quantum Age, we may eventually call them "alternate recollections," indicating awareness of the fact that we know that each and every one of us exists in a superimposed state, with access to many possible alternate histories, presents, and futures.

Ulric Neisser and Nicole Harsch conducted studies of Emory University students' accuracy of recollections of events at the time of the *Challenger* space shuttle explosion, starting by collecting first-hand accounts from 106 students the day after the disaster detailing how they'd heard of the explosion, what they'd been doing at the time, where they were, and how they felt. The researchers followed up with the same students two and a half years later, and were startled to find that students achieved a mean score of 2.95 compared to a perfect score of 7. Less than 10% of the students were able to exactly match their original recollection of events, and over half of the students got a score less than 2.

The most noteworthy findings in this "flashbulb" memory study were student reactions when confronted with conflicting accounts. Many students persisted in confidently claiming that their current memories of events were completely accurate, even when confronted with their own hand-written journal entries. One student summed up what happened succinctly, *"That's my handwriting, but that's not what happened."*

It's important to note that in this new Quantum Age, such cases of alternate histories are to be expected. They provide evidence of the superposition of states that we and everything around us exists within, so we can expect to occasionally see documented records from the past that differ from what we recall. In the Quantum Age, we understand that seeing our own handwritten notes that aren't at all what we remember is one way that alternate histories become known.

Entangled Diamonds & Altruistic Rats

Scientific discoveries in one field often have parallel findings in other fields, as witnessed in the case of results from the fascinating diamond entanglement study arriving at the same point in time as neurobiologists are citing the significance of empathy and altruism in animals—such as jailbreak rats that spring their pals and share sweets.

At first glance, entangled diamonds and altruistic rats don't seem to have much in common, yet once we've taken a closer look, we begin to see how in a universe where everything exists as vibration, some vibrations occur harmonically across space and time in ways that resonance is achieved and information is exchanged.

On the physics front, recent groundbreaking experiments at the Clarendon Laboratory at the University of Oxford in England have successfully demonstrated that two physically separated diamonds vibrated together when only one of them was zapped with an ultrashort laser. This kind of entanglement previously has been witnessed only at the quantum level... beyond reach of our ordinary range of sensory perception. What's so exciting about these experiments is how they move the mysteriously exotic world of quantum mechanics into our everyday world of objects we can touch, taste, smell, hear and feel.

Quantum entanglement is one of those strange behaviors that physicist Albert Einstein once referred to as "spooky action at a distance," and like quantum teleportation and quantum tunneling, quantum entanglement is something seldom acknowledged on the macroscopic scale. Scientific successes in observing "quantum weirdness" with things larger than quantum particles are initiating a paradigm shift to better assumptions about our world. Some of the new assumptions about the nature of reality include: the energy of things matters as much as the material; non-local effects can be profound; observers influence experimental results; and some outcomes are best described in terms of probabilities.

Diamonds were selected for the Oxford entanglement study for their crystalline nature... yet we see evidence of the biological equivalent of entanglement in many places, including in neurons. Over the past decade, some neurological researchers have suggested a theory that the presence of mirror neurons might help explain empathy, since some neurologists see evidence supporting the possibility that mirror neurons enable a person to know how someone feels by watching them, allowing that person to literally feel what they are feeling. Psychologists often conduct psychology experiments with rats, which have a special place in my heart, as my daughters raised pet rats when they were young and we learned first-hand what wonderful pets they make.

Rats are highly intelligent social creatures that can form strong bonds with other rats and people, as my daughters and I learned one day when our lost pet rat came bounding home after four days out in the world on her own. While I was amazed that our pet rat survived four days on her own, my daughter explained that she'd never lost confidence in her rat returning, because, *"I told her to come back home, and she did."*

Another thing I learned from having rats as pets is that rats are socially conscious beings that behave compassionately for others. The exciting news from recent experiments with rats comes from University of Chicago neuroscientists Peggy Mason, Inbal Ben-Ami Bartal, and Jean Decety who conducted an experiment with rats in which rats had an opportunity to free a rat trapped in a plexiglass cage. Amazingly, a majority of the rats learned how to open the cage and free the other rat, and did so of their own volition. Rats did not free similarly caged toy rats, demonstrating they knew the difference between someone who was suffering and an inanimate object. When given a dilemma between opening a locked cage containing special chocolate treats and freeing a trapped rat, rats typically chose to first free the trapped rat and then access the treats, rather than ensuring they got more treats for themselves.

"In our lab we called it the 'chocolate versus pal'
experiment," Mason says. "The rat could have put his butt

in the opening of the cage containing chocolate to block the other guy, but he didn't. They were sharing food with their pals. In rat land, that is big—I was shocked."

The implications of these entangled diamonds and altruistic rat studies are truly profound, as it's clear that we are now entering a time when we can feel awe and wonder at witnessing *"some of the strange effects observable in the microscopic world"* that Dr. Dean Radin presciently predicted we'd encounter. We are now officially invited to re-envision a more unified universe in which we may be more and better connected to one another than we've ever previously conceived possible.

Rubidium Teleportation

A huge breakthrough occurred in November 2012, when a team of scientists led by Xiao-Hui Bao at the University of Science and Technology of China in Hefei reported the first ever successful teleportation between two macroscopic objects —bundles of rubidium atoms—across a distance of almost 150 meters, using entangled photons to transmit information that remained stable for just 100 microseconds.

In June 2013, a team of physicists led by Eugene Polzik succeeded in consistently teleporting information between two sealed glass vials of cesium gas at the Niels Bohr Institute at the University of Copenhagen in Denmark.

What's so significant about these successful macro-scale teleportations is that long-held conceptual boundaries between what was considered possible and impossible are blurring, as we develop techniques to move quantum behaviors into our everyday world.

Birds Do It, Plants Do It

Those who expect modern human technology to be faster and more efficient than the rustic natural world are quite surprised to learn that our best photovoltaic cells are only 20% efficient, compared with photosynthesizing plants and bacteria that regularly achieve 95% efficiency rates for transforming sunlight into energy. Plants have existed on Earth for millions of years, so it's not too surprising to find that their natural process of photosynthesis likely utilizes quantum coherence to speed things up. In decades past, scientists believed that excited electrons carried energy randomly through photosynthetic systems in plants, hopping from one molecule to the next. More modern measurements of energy in the new field of quantum biology studying photosynthesizing plants indicates something much more efficient is going on. What appears to be happening is that electrons take advantage of the fact that energy can move not just in the material form, but in pure energy form, too, and entire systems of molecules can become entangled to allow the formation of a coherent wave that tries out different pathways simultaneously, until the most efficient route is very quickly determined. The quantum magic happens in each of a photosynthetic cell's millions of antenna proteins that are surprisingly efficient and robust at routing energy with very little lost in transit.

University of Toronto biophysicist Greg Scholes published his findings of room-temperature quantum coherence behavior in common marine algae in *Nature*. Scholes describes an analogy of driving home through rush hour traffic to explain what these cells are doing:

> *"... you have three ways of driving home through rush hour traffic. On any given day, you take only one. You don't know if the other routes would be quicker or slower. But in quantum mechanics, you can take all three of these routes simultaneously. You don't specify where you are until you arrive, so you always choose the quickest route."*

Plants aren't the only natural systems enjoying the benefits of quantum living; birds appear to be navigating by Earth's geomagnetic fields thanks to compass cells that make use of quantum physical processes, too. Magnetoreception is the name of the ability of some migrating species to navigate with assistance from the Earth's magnetic field. It's long been a mystery how birds can navigate apparently utilizing magnetism of the Earth. While some scientists theorized there might be a magnetite-based mechanism helping birds navigate by means of an inner compass, experiments with European robins disproved that hypothesis. European robins have a magnetic sense, yet they didn't demonstrate the type of polarity sensitivities that would have been expected.

Surprisingly, what does appear to be assisting birds with their wonderful sense of direction is something almost nobody would have suspected. A series of behavioral experiments has demonstrated that the birds' navigation sense was photoreceptor based—dependent on the presence of certain frequencies of ambient light. Avian magnetic sensors appear to be activated by light striking the bird's retina, with their sense of direction working much better in daytime rather than at night. Researchers postulate that energy deposited by each photon creates pairs of free radicals—highly reactive molecules—that each have an unpaired electron. These unpaired electrons are easily influenced by magnetic fields, so as the radicals separate, one is more influenced by the pull of the Earth's magnetic field than the other, which shifts the pair of free radicals between two quantum states that have different chemical reactivity.

Quantum Teleportation in Our Sense of Smell

In the field of quantum biology, some scientists including Dr. Luca Turin of the Fleming Institute in Greece suspect that many of the processes we've known about for years may have at their very heart a quantum basis. As a matter of fact, one leading possible example of quantum teleportation in the field of biology is as close as the nose on your face! According to the quantum tunneling explanation, aromatic molecules wiggle and vibrate in such a way that electrons in the olfactory receptors of our noses disappear on one side of a fragrant molecule and reappear on the other. This idea of quantum smelling has been gaining ground recently, since it explains why molecules that include sulfur and hydrogen atoms bonded together can take a wide variety of shapes, yet no matter which way these molecules combine, our nose scent receptors invariably register that familiar rotten egg smell every time. Dr. Turin explains,

> *"If you look from the standpoint of an alternative theory —that what determines the smell of a molecule is the vibrations—the sulphur-hydrogen mystery becomes absolutely clear."*

When energy of just the right frequency causes collections of atoms to vibrate, these spring-like collections of atoms vibrate every time an electron in a particularly "smelly" molecule jumps or tunnels across the receptor, simultaneously depositing a quantum of energy into one of the molecule's bonds, which sets the springy group of atoms in that molecule vibrating.

Quantum Biology Reveals Entangled Beings

Recent experiments have found many macro-scale examples such as birds, plants, and salt crystals exhibiting signs of being entangled with one another. Such entanglement appears to be a quality of quantum behavior that we can claim for ourselves and for our connections in the form of synchronization with our pets, plants, and animals.

English biologist Dr. Rupert Sheldrake, former research fellow of the Royal Society, has studied and reported on case studies involving more than 500 dogs who knew when their owners were coming home—even when such returns were spontaneous, rather than scheduled. Sheldrake also makes note of animals finding their people far away, and demonstrating foreknowledge of impending dangers we wouldn't expect them to have advance knowledge of, such as a foot trail that has unexpectedly washed out just ahead, or an owner's otherwise unexpected sudden death.

In the United States of America, Cleve Backster conducted numerous experiments that recorded how clearly his "pet" plants responded to his spontaneous decisions to return to his laboratory. Backster worked with the galvanic skin response portion of his polygraph "lie detection" equipment, connecting it to plants in his office to track their responses to a variety of test situations. Amazingly, the plants responded immediately with clear reactions squiggled in polygraph ink at every exact moment he made a decision to come back to his lab.

The fact that plants and animals we are familiar with are so attuned to what we are spontaneously deciding to do, even when we may be miles away and just came to that decision on impulse, whimsy, or random choice has staggering implications. There is clearly a level of interconnectedness between each and every one of us at work, in our neighborhoods, in our families, with our friends, and with all the plants and animals we feel closest to.

Why Do People Quantum Jump?

There are as many reasons to experience quantum jumping as there are people in the world, with people from all walks of life enjoying the benefits of making a sudden leap to a new reality. Feel like you missed your calling? Quantum jumping allows you to explore your interest and passions, and feel you are living a life that more truly reflects your true identity. Want to live a richer life? Quantum jumping can give you a feeling of being more lucidly aware—like being awake inside a dream, and finding it's possible to instantly change yourself and your situation. Ready for a fresh start? Quantum jumping can provide you with ways to escape unpleasant situations in many ways—from miraculous healing to superhuman strength. Some people quantum jump to become happier, healthier, wealthier or wiser, to find love or like-minded friends, or to rapidly and easily acquire a variety of skills and abilities. Quantum jumping can also come in wonderfully handy in times of emergency when you can benefit from being teleported to safety, or "tunneling" safely through an oncoming vehicle.

Quantum Jumping to Find Lost Things

Quantum jumping can be a wonderful way to find lost things. The value of quantum jumping for finding lost things becomes more evident when you've lost something of great personal importance. When you contemplate the possibility that there is more than one of everything—which most physicists today agree is true, in the sense that everything exists in a superposition of all possible states—then you can readily envision a reality in which you are reunited with something that's been lost, stolen, or misplaced. Keep an open mind to seeing what's been lost returning to you at some point, and feel how much you love it without worrying overly much that it's gone in order to experience best results.

Quantum Jumping to Find Love

Whether you'd like to find that special someone to date or marry, or some friends who see you for who you are and are fun to hang out with, it's possible to envision any or all of these things for yourself, and jump into those realities. Quantum jumping can help you meet the types of people you most enjoy, and do what it takes to improve your relationships once you're in them—by imagining you are seeing your best possible relationship self involved in healthy, respectful relationships with people who love being with you as much as you love being with them.

If you're already in a romantic relationship, but the honeymoon feels like it's over, you can make a quantum jump into a relationship with your current partner where you feel much more compassionate and connected. You and your partner can instantly feel improvement in love, passion, and intimacy, so both of you can enjoy a second honeymoon.

Quantum Jumping to Lose Weight

You can employ quantum jumping to lose weight by envisioning regular actions you'll need in your new daily routine for achieving and maintaining a healthy weight, and sticking to it. This might involve feeling inspired to be more active, choosing smaller snacks with fewer sugars and carbohydrates, and drinking more water, for example. There are many ways to ensure success, all of which depend on your first feeling enthused about the possibility of a newer, healthier, thinner you. There are weight loss groups and calorie counting websites you can join, hypnosis programs you can sign up for, and self-hypnosis books you can read.

And if you want to literally get jumping, you can practice rebounding—a playful form of low-impact cardio exercise you can do on a miniature trampoline! Jumping on low-to-the-floor rebounders is easy on the joints, while working all the muscle groups in your body. You gain advantages when quantum jumping to lose weight from suddenly feeling inspired to make positive changes in your life, and from getting to know yourself as a healthier, slimmer, more physically fit you.

Quantum Jumping for Career Success

People who are feeling trapped, hemmed in, or concerned that there's no way forward are prime candidates for experiencing quantum jumps at work and in their careers. Whether you're longing for promotion, transfer, or an entirely new job in a completely new field, quantum jumping is a valuable technique for moving onward and upward, and for getting unstuck.

Quantum jumping can help you feel more confident, less stressed, and better able to develop and nurture the supportive relationships required to ensure your professional success. You can overcome a tendency toward procrastination, gain necessary willpower, gain perseverance, and develop powers of persuasion and negotiation you've never had before. You can quantum jump into a reality where you not only feel happier internally, but are also better liked and appreciated by those around you.

Quantum Jumping to Improve Physical Performance

Some of the most successful sports coaches in the world evoke award-winning performance from their teams by instructing athletes to act as if they are the best at what they strive to do. All of us—even non-athletes—can benefit from improved balance, agility, stamina, and strength.

Quantum jumping can enhance every aspect of physicality, from physical endurance to insensitivity to pain. You can become less accident-prone while enjoying a new level of confidence from improved grace and dexterity... all because you believe and act as if these are qualities you fully possess. You can inspire not just yourself, but those around you, too, as you demonstrate a positive attitude toward everything you do.

Quantum Jumping for Better Health

One of the most common reasons for people to make a quantum jump is for better health. Sometimes people experience spontaneous remissions of cancer or disease without medical intervention in ways that are truly amazing. I've known many people whose tumors and cancer have undergone spontaneous remission, and have also heard from people whose pets have experienced seemingly miraculous cures.

I've made a quantum jump from a state of not being able to breathe due to asthma to breathing just fine, making asthma a thing of the past. This memorable event occurred many years ago while I was in an exercise class, attempting to keep up with the group, when I found myself suddenly unable to breathe. Thinking quickly and remembering a simple qigong exercise practiced by energy practitioners and shamans around the world, I scooped up two handfuls of energy (which looked to observers like two hands full of air) and brought them inward toward my chest. I imagined I was bringing in positive Qi—positive energy—and repeated the process a few more times. Almost instantaneously I was able to breathe just fine, and haven't had a recurrence of asthma since.

Quantum Jumping for Money

Have you ever noticed how some people seem to have a knack for coming into just the right amount of money at exactly the right time? If this sounds like an appealing scenario to you, then quantum jumps involving money are likely something you'll enjoy experiencing now and again.

When you jump into a reality in which the money you need is already yours, you experience the joys of witnessing money that sometimes seems to literally come from thin air. I describe numerous such occasions in my book, *RealityShifters Guide to*

High Energy Money, noting that often we get exactly the amount of money we really need. There's advantage in developing and maintaining a playful, fun sense of enthusiasm when moving into realities where you have the money you need, and taking positive action to do good things in the world helps tremendously, too.

Quantum Jumps to Survive Emergencies

Life-or-death situations aren't something most people plan for every day, yet it's easy to recognize the importance of instantaneously being able to access previously untapped abilities in emergency situations. In an emergency when a jack stand falls over and drops a 2,000 pound car on a loved one, we can appreciate how some people have harnessed superhuman strength to save someone's life. When some people have been trapped in sub-zero temperatures in the wilderness, they've tapped into yogi-like abilities to attain a near hibernation state until help arrived. In addition to situations where lives are at stake, some people make quantum jumps during times of spiritual emergencies while feeling emotionally bogged down, or when feeling no sense of joy or purpose.

Some of the most commonly reported teleportation experiences reported to me through my RealityShifters web site have occurred during near collisions with oncoming vehicles. Numerous people have shared stories with me of seeing a fast-moving car or truck bearing down on them at a time and place where they had nowhere to go... and then a split-second later, either the oncoming vehicle was now on the other side of them without any sign of a crash, or they found themselves instantaneously transported to safety. Such first-hand accounts are remarkable to me for so clearly falling into these two general categories (the oncoming vehicle is now safely on the other side, or the experiencer was teleported to safety) in ways that closely mirror types of quantum behavior. In case of emergency, take a moment to blip out of physical material form into pure energy until it's safe to return, or teleport to a safer location.

Quantum Jumps to Explore True Identity

In her book, *Future Memory,* PMH Atwater writes, *"Future memory registers in the mind as if a segment of physical reality was just experienced in its complete entirety—as if the future had unfolded in the present."*

Future memories are terrific guideposts for helping us select between parallel possible realities even as they are beginning to unfold before us, welcoming us to walk forward as if on red carpets rolling out from this decision point right here and now. When we get a glimpse, for example, of a possible reality in which our luggage has been stolen... or in which we find a beautiful ring in a consignment shop and we sense we've seen these possible futures before, we can begin to play with the knowledge that we've seen and visited these other realities or other possible futures before. I've had both types of future memory occur while on a trip to southern California. Thanks to being tipped off to possible theft, I was able to prevent loss. Thanks to a future memory of finding a ring in a consignment shop, I found a lovely piece of jewelry I'd not have otherwise discovered.

It's clear that the age-old debate about fate/determinism versus free will is one that will carry on, but the place I sense resolution to it lies in the realms we visit in dreams and know to be our true selves who are eternal, infinite, and multifaceted. On that level of self, in which we are more like "I AM" big self than small "me" ego selves, we know we are all as One, we comprehend the biggest picture view of the multiverse, and we have a much deeper appreciation for the meaning of all that sometimes seems so meaningless in our lives.

Quantum Jumps to Feel More Spiritual, Lucid, & Aware

For spiritually focused individuals, quantum jumping holds the promise of attaining an optimal state of lucid living awareness in which one becomes aware of living a waking dream, while attaining an energized, grounded state of consciousness. With such a conscious approach, it's possible to utilize the benefits of reality shifts without running afoul of the dangers of overly narrow-focused reality shifting in which one gets what one asked for, to great dismay. Quantum jumping can thus be seen to ultimately be a spiritual path, in the sense that its practice can teach us compassion, empathy and kindness when we see ourselves as part of the interconnectedness of all that is.

Another way that quantum jumping can be a spiritual practice is that we can learn from experience that to focus first on manifesting what one thinks one wants before knowing what best to ask for is pretty much always putting the cart before the horse. The ways I know that work best for people in general to experience reality shifts and quantum jumps are thus based on attaining states of emotional or energetic awareness in order to engage in a dialogue with the multiverse, rather than strictly adhering to pre-formulated rigid steps.

Quantum jumping can provide a means for learning about our world, our universe, and our multiverse. We are living in a truly exciting time right now, when for the first time in human history, we are seeing quantum behavior on the macroscopic scale. It's clear that humanity is poised to get some traction regarding which of the quantum interpretations hold the most 'water.' We might see confirmation in our lifetimes for one or more of the quantum interpretation theories, which I find completely thrilling.

Quantum Jumps to Teleport Ourselves

When you first heard the term "quantum jumping," one image that came to mind might have been of people teleporting instantaneously around the world, experiencing other worlds of possibility. Even as progress in quantum physics and quantum biology laboratories moves steadily forward, we'll likely still have a bit of a wait before we see anything like William Shatner playing Captain Kirk on *Star Trek*, saying his famous line into his communicator, *"Kirk to Enterprise. Beam us up, Scotty."* Aside from earlier mentioned survival in emergency situations, most people aren't experiencing teleportation whenever they wish to make jumps to other places and times.

While reading an article, "Living in a Quantum World," in *Scientific American* recently, I was heartened to see the article's subtitle, "Quantum mechanics is not just about teeny particles, it applies to things of all sizes: birds, plants, maybe even people." We are truly living in wonderful times as we see mainstream scientific articles acknowledging that quantum mechanics applies to everything in the universe—-even ourselves. What this means for our expanding world view is that we can expect to see signs of such things as quantum entanglement, quantum teleportation, and quantum tunneling around us in everyday life —with no need for electron microscopes.

The *Scientific American* article, "Living in a Quantum World" states,

> *"In a quantum world, a particle does not just have to take one path at a time; it can take all of them simultaneously."*

One implication of this idea of quantum behavior showing up on the macroscopic scale includes the notion that there is more than one of everything. Sometimes, we can expect to see signs of alternate worlds around us as things and people transform, transport, disappear, and reappear. These signs can clue us in to the possibility that we are surrounded by an infinite number of parallel universes that, on some level, we are experiencing in their totality.

Learning to Allow Quantum Jumps

Asking why we'd want to quantum jump takes us directly to the front lines of the question of our true identity, and the debate over who we think we are... raising the philosophical question of how we feel about free will versus destiny. Put more simply, the very idea of quantum jumping brings us head-to-head with our own beliefs about who we are, what we experience, and who and what we're capable of being and experiencing. People who think it's not possible to quantum jump will more likely have trouble doing it, though this book is designed to help readers enjoy quantum jumping success by sharing real-life examples of the growing scientific evidence of quantum jumping on a macroscopic scale, as well as practical steps for how to quantum jump.

In the first chapter of this book, we got a better understanding of what quantum jumping is all about. In Chapter Two, we've explored why people quantum jump. Chapter Three will provide steps for how to quantum jump, and Chapter Four shares exciting real-life examples of quantum jumps. *Quantum Jumps* is designed to help you open your mind to new beliefs about the nature of reality, and the range of possible realities you can focus on, energize, and choose to live within.

Why do beliefs matter? Those who believe the brain is the mind, and consciousness cannot possibly exist beyond the brain constrain themselves to a materialistic paradigm which presents obstacles to successfully experiencing and recognizing quantum jumping. From this worldview, free will is limited by necessity to addressing only matters within one's direct control, so those with such beliefs conclude there cannot exist outside of oneself anything that could possibly influence us.

Those who believe consciousness is non-local and unlimited, with ability to communicate information instantaneously across time and space are open to experiencing and recognizing quantum jumping. From such a worldview, free will can be viewed on a level of ego identity (relating to one's mortal physical self) and also to a sense of being part of the overall collective all-that-is.

In actuality, best results will likely be obtained by those who have *no* beliefs at all. There can be a beautiful balance between intentional, active manifesting—in which what is desired and expected is clearly envisioned and held firmly in mind—and in allowing ourselves to receive whatever comes our way. Numerous studies have shown that refraining from over-thinking (or over-believing) is an important success factor in life, mostly because people who don't become paralyzed with worry and over-thinking are more likely to try new things, take more risks, and enjoy more opportunities.

You might be suffering from "analysis paralysis" if you obsess over things you have little or no control over. "Analysis paralysis" refers to the unhappy state in which a person is so busy comparing various options and possible outcomes in pursuit of an ever-elusive "perfect" or optimal solutions that no action is actually taken. Worries and fears take hold, and there is a sense that perfection can never be attained. Essentially, what gets in the way for those suffering from such concerns is Ego, with people becoming overwhelmed with fear of failure or loss, rather than being inspired and motivated by hopeful new possibilities. You can learn to trust your gut feelings and intuition, try new things, and accept that you're not perfect and don't need to become perfect.

When we understand that our belief structures are creations of our minds, we start noticing how varied individual belief structures can be from person to person. What one person considers to be realistic and matter-of-fact might seem outrageously peculiar to another. Even the idea that other people actually *see* images in their minds may seem outlandish to some people, let alone what those people see. When enough people shift their belief structures to look at the world in fresh, new ways, cultural paradigms shift.

Staying current with new scientific findings can help. While most non-physicists would likely see a solid physical object such as a table or a chair as only what it currently appears to be, a remarkable 2/3 majority of physicists interviewed in 2011 stated they believe that *all* objects can exist in superimposed states—much the way we know quantum 'particles' exist as energetic probabilities as much as physical particles we can measure and observe. University of Portland, Oregon, physics professor, Maximilian Schlosshauer summarized this remarkable agreement thus,

> *"More than two-thirds believed that there is no fundamental limit to quantum theory—that it should be possible for objects, no matter how big, to be prepared in quantum superpositions like Schrödinger's cat. So the era where quantum theory was associated only with the atomic realm appears finally over."*

While this particular debate may have ended for physicists, such a worldview of all physical objects existing in superpositions of states—like Schrödinger's cat being both alive and dead at the same time—may take a while to be fully adopted by the public at large. This new concept of reality for the dawning Quantum Age helps us recognize that what happens in the quantum realm not only doesn't stay in the quantum realm—it affects everything. Applying quantum logic to history gives us the new field of Alternate Histories. Applying quantum logic to legal systems instigates an overhaul of criminal and civil law. Applying quantum logic to the field of medicine demands recognition of the placebo effect and spontaneous remission as completely natural occurrences that can be better facilitated.

When I contemplate all the possible me's that I can be, and the idea that right now I have full access to so many ways of living, being, and expressing myself, I feel a sense of wonder and awe. This concept of quantum jumping to parallel realities gives me a feeling of having access to a fresh new start at any given point in time, and a joyful feeling of gratitude for being alive in this new Quantum Age!

*   *   *

Now that we've gained a better idea why we'd want to experience quantum jumps, the next chapter, *Changing Past, Present and Future,* describes a simple three-step process we can use to start making quantum jumps today!

Exercise

Free Will and True Identity Perspective

Imagine yourself viewing your life in advance before you were born. Imagine making choices before coming into the world regarding: which country you'll arrive in, what year, month, day and hour you'll be born, and who your mother and father will be. Envision yourself recognizing multitudes of challenges and opportunities in this wondrous life, and making some choices ahead of time with certain signs and signals you'll be sure to recognize even when ensconced in the experience of living your life. Imagine how many possibilities are left open, so you can better come to know your true identity as you make choices that help you develop inner confidence and overcome your fears.

Exercise

Experiencing the Quantum Realm

Sensing the Smallest & Largest

While breathing slowly and deeply, touch the tips of your thumbs to the tips of your pinky fingers on both hands so they just barely meet; feel a tingle of energy flowing between finger and thumb. Breathe deeply, and touch the tip of your thumbs to the tips of your ring fingers. Now, touch the tips of your thumbs to your middle fingers. Next, touch the tips of your big fingers to the tips of your thumbs. Continue breathing deeply and fully, and close your eyes as you again touch the tips of your thumbs to the tips of your pinky fingers. Imagine as you do this that you bring together the very small consciousness that is what you think of as "me" with the "I Am" oneness consciousness of All That Is, sending all that positive knowingness through your body and being.

Exercise

Encourage Premonitory Visions

Research suggests those who are most open to new experiences and capable of being deeply ensconced in and focused upon a given activity are likely to experience premonitions... and openness to a certain degree of chaos helps, too. You can encourage visions of possible futures as Dr. Larry Dossey suggests in his book, *The Power of Premonitions* when you, "... court difference, variety and ambiguity in your life. Relax and let go. Don't try too hard. Give up your pet ideas of how the world *should* work." Foster such openness to full awareness by practicing mindfulness meditation in which you promise yourself that every time a certain occurrence happens—such as any time you hear a bird sing—you will close your eyes and meditate, however briefly, clearing your mind and paying attention to the bird song while taking slow, deep, rhythmic breaths.

Exercise

Why Do You Want to Quantum Jump?

If you could jump into any possible reality... which one would you choose? Close your eyes and envision a reality you'd most like to enjoy. Picture where you are, how you look, what you sound like, how you dress, how you behave, who you're with and what you're doing. Pay attention to every detail, noting what makes this reality special. If you see the other you in a loving relationship, notice how you interact. If the other you loves their work, pay attention to what activities are involved. Write down everything you see about this possible you, intending that you'll get continuing guidance and inspiration from this other you.

"Whatever you do,
or dream you can, begin it.
Boldness has genius and power
and magic in it."
— *Johann Wolfgang von Goethe*

Chapter 3

Changing Past, Present, & Future

There was something magical about watching my first child learning to walk one warm summer night in a town square in Austria. She'd been working her way up to the big moment for months, pulling herself up to standing alongside tables and chairs several times a day, and had finally established enough balance to tentatively rise up from squatting to standing. On the day she took her first steps there was a twinkle in her eyes, and a bounce in her hips as she practiced her new trick of standing up and sitting down—sometimes quite abruptly. My parents and husband and I were visiting the beautiful town of Abtenau, enjoying dinner at one of the sidewalk cafés around the cobblestone church square, listening to lively polka music played on electrified instruments by musicians in traditional folk dress. At one point when my daughter rose to standing, some elderly diners at a nearby table cheered her on, applauding... and we saw her start to walk! Something about the warm atmosphere, encouraging audience and festive music gave her a visible energy boost as she moved one foot in front of the other and took her very first steps.

To those of us who have been walking for many years, such a simple achievement as learning to walk may not seem like much, since we've forgotten how many times we fell down and got back up to try again. There is an advantage in persistence, and in holding fast to a vision of something being doable, even though you've never done it before.

You Can Jump if You Want To

If you can walk, you can dance—and you can quantum jump. Your body is designed for quantum jumping, so learning how to improve your skills can be every bit as simple as making the transition from walking to dancing. The essential spirit of quantum jumping might be summed up in American psychologist William James' words,

"If you want a quality, act as if you already have it."

Sounds simple enough, right? Well, as you might have suspected, sometimes there can be a little more to it than that. If we were perfectly now-centric beings, with no worries for the future or regrets and misgivings about the past, quantum jumping would be much easier, for the simple reason that we'd all be experiencing the benefits of having beginner's minds. The challenges of jumping to a new reality become clear when we start doubting ourselves based on who we think we are based on what we've already done and what we think we can do. These areas are outside the realm of the eternal now, yet most people who don't practice mindfulness tend to worry a fair bit about the future and the past. When we're not mindful, it's easy to get caught up in drama triangles in which we feel like we've been victimized, or like there is a "bad guy" or that we need to rescue someone. What we need, in other words, is the ability to focus exclusively on who we'd most like to be and what we most need to be doing, without getting caught up in all the drama we're so used to in our everyday lives. Here's where we can gain some insight from those who study the nature of reality and consciousness in the fields of neuroscience and physics.

Neuroscientist Gregor Thut of the Institute of Neuroscience and Psychology observes,

"Despite experiencing the world as a continuum, we do not sample our world continuously but in discrete snapshots determined by the cycles of brain rhythms."

Quantum jumping takes advantage of these usually unseen discontinuities, so we can make a leap from one reality to another as smoothly as walking through the one we're already in. And one of the more interesting aspects of quantum jumping is that in addition to making a leap to a parallel reality, we're making changes to our futures and our pasts. You've felt such changes happen to your future and your past any time you've felt increased hope for your future or gratitude for your past... as doubts, worries, regrets and fears slipped away. As H.G. Wells said in the movie *The Time Machine*,

"We all have our time machines, don't we. Those that take us back are memories... and those that carry us forward are dreams."

But what if making a leap to a better reality could be easy? What if we could get help to stay balanced and take our first steps in a new direction when we need it? When we consider the Transactional Interpretation of quantum physics where there's a "handshake" between a possible future point in space-time and now, we see something amazingly special going on. There is every bit as much involvement from the future point in space-time reaching back to you as there is from you reaching forward for that "brass ring." Why is imagining a future You that is reaching back and giving you a hand up so important?

Because it makes the study of quantum jumps so much easier. You don't need to make such a huge effort. It's just as important to relax, raise your confidence and Qi (internal energy) to a level where you feel closely aligned with your desired future reality.

In June 2006, dozens of scholars traveled from all around the world to gather in San Diego, California at the "Frontiers of Time: Retrocausation—Experiment and Theory" physics symposium. This very special section of the 87th annual meeting of the Pacific Division of the American Association for the Advancement of Science (AAAS) was convened for the purpose of examining the nature of time... and causality. Conference organizer and University of San Diego physicist Daniel Sheehan explains,

> "To say that it's impossible for the future to influence the past is to deny half of the predictions of the laws of physics."

Despite the fact that no clear consensus viewpoint yet exists amongst leading researchers in the field of reverse causation (also known as backward causation or retro-causation) as to just how, exactly, the future can influence the past, most physicists do accept the idea of time symmetry. *"The tendency is to ignore it, to say it's just a fact of nature that time moves one way,"* said physicist Michael Ibison from the University of Texas at Austin. Daniel Sheehan agrees,

> "People know how to calculate with quantum mechanics, but that's not to say they know what it means. Quantum mechanics is like poetry. The poem is right there, for everyone to see, but it has many different interpretations."

While University of Washington physicist John Cramer awaits positive results from his experiment to detect photons of light before they've been emitted, the best current evidence for reverse causation comes from the field of parapsychology, where experiments are being conducted to investigate such things as telepathy, clairvoyance, precognition, psychokinesis and other types of psi phenomena. While growing numbers of studies in the field of parapsychology, such as those by UC Berkeley physicist Henry Stapp, indicate experimental participants are able to influence radioactive decay of isotopes in the past, few mainstream research laboratories are repeating these experiments.

> *"You'd think people would want to either refute or confirm some of these reports,"* said Stapp, *"but the only people willing to test them are people who already tend to believe them. Most mainstream labs shy away for fear of sullying their reputations, as if they would be dirtying their hands by even imagining some of this is possible."*

Who are our quantum jumping experts? We can look to our top athletes, medical miracle people who've experienced spontaneous remissions of otherwise incurable medical conditions, and our top businessmen and women. We can also learn from survivors who've experienced life-saving miracles, heroes who have acted courageously by "just doing what needed to be done," people who've had near death experiences (NDEs), experienced meditators, and people who've worked with lucid dreams, daydreams and hypnosis to access other realities.

If you've sometimes recalled alternate histories—something like a different ending to a book or movie, or perhaps you've been surprised to hear recent news about certain celebrity when you clearly remember seeing reports of their death—then you have already quantum jumped.

One of the important keys to success is knowing that there is much more than just one universe. There are many more than just two realities. You can think of what's happening as a large number of possible realities co-existing in a blur of energy waves at every decision point. Amidst all these possible realities, there are some realities you are much more likely to find enjoyable and meaningful.

Three Steps to Quantum Jumps

The following three steps to achieving quantum jumps are meditative in nature, so they tend to work best either while in quiet contemplation, or in a daydreamy or hypnotic state. If you have access to a recording device and earphones, you can create your own guided journey through the three steps, playing it back as you fall asleep each night, or during a peaceful time of day when you can close your eyes and completely relax.

People who experience miracles are described in Carolyn Miller's book as creating the right conditions for miracles by attaining a detached and peaceful altered state, expecting a positive rather than negative outcome, and focusing on love rather than fear with a changed perception of what had been viewed as the problem. Carolyn Miller defines a miracle as: "... an instance in which a supernatural power interferes in the natural world," which sounds a lot like quantum jumps or reality shifts to me. As it turns out, the three steps of miracle-mindedness are similar to three steps for successful quantum jumps.

Quantum Jumping Steps

(1) Attain a relaxed, detached and peaceful altered state.

(2) Feel energized about your visualized positive outcome.

(3) Take positive action in keeping with your new reality.

Step One: Attain A Detached, Peaceful State of Mind

While you might think of achieving goals in terms of being active and doing things, one surprising truth about quantum jumps is that despite the name, "quantum jump," there's not so much action involved in the jumping as one might think. The required state before making a leap to another reality is more like being *in between* states—in the midst of a nice daydream— than making a big effort or exertion. You can access such a detached state of mind through meditation, or lucid dreaming.

This sense of peaceful detachment is vitally important, because this state of mind allows us to let go of the conscious, ego-driven mindset that got us into whatever challenging situations we are presently engaged. We must *let go* of what we think is best and believe should occur, so we can maintain a neutral, receptive state of mind. The energy of charged emotions tends to lock realities and particular histories in place —so it's essential that we attain a state of emotional and energetic detachment that allows us to calmly respond to whatever comes next.

We can experience mindful harmonious balance when we appreciate our many possible pasts and futures with gratitude and love, rather than regrets and fears. Meditating at such a point of emotional balance and detachment helps us naturally achieve internal attitudinal adjustments, which in turn help us make better choices, that we won't regret later on.

The key to meditation is mindful awareness. There are many ways to attain a detached, peaceful state of mind in meditation, including: walking meditation, breathing meditation, silent meditation, chanting meditation, meditating while gardening, meditating while bathing, or meditating doing dishes or chores.

Just as Asian cultures respect the complementary dynamics of Yin (feminine) and Yang (masculine), the first step in quantum jumping can be thought of as a meditative Zen-like acceptance of all that is, while internally "going to our happy place." This is a Yin quality of receptivity that appears to be the opposite of action. If you are experiencing the multiverse like a quantum particle, this state of detached receptivity feels like letting go of your material nature so you no longer fixate on any given point in space-time, and instead spread yourself out in the form of pure energy waves across all possible realities. In such a state of being pure energy, you can envision all possible futures and pasts, and quickly see where each choice ends up.

Can you imagine that you and everything and everyone around you exists in a superposition of states? When we achieve a peaceful, detached state of mind, it's analogous to the kind of superposition of all possibilities that a majority of physicists agreed is true for everything—not just tiny quantum particles. It is possible to contemplate that we can make the best decisions when remembering that in a multiverse of many possible worlds, everything can happen—and actually is happening—somewhere. In order to arrive at a preferred reality, we must first disengage and detach from our daily struggles by taking a meditative break in the peaceful feeling of calm we experience at the center of all options.

Quantum jumping is very much like shifting gears. When we change gears while driving a car with a stick-shift, we move out of one particular reality—such as first gear—by first deselecting all gears as we put our foot on the clutch pedal. From that place of accessing all possibilities, we can move to the next reality we select—such as second gear. Being conscious of existing in such a superposition of states is akin to being in a state of timelessness... a feeling of being detached from, rather than attached to, everyday reality. From meditating or dreaming in such a timeless place of pure energetic being, we can calmly focus on exactly what we'd most prefer to happen next before returning to our regular mindset and our preferred reality.

Step Two: Feel Energized About Visualized Outcome

Studies confirm that athletes perform considerably better after first visualizing success. More specifically, the top athletes depend on mental practice or imagery rehearsal of doing what it takes to be their best in order to help guarantee their winning edge. When athletes first practice their maneuvers in their imagination before actual physical performances, studies consistently show they benefit from improvements in skill, confidence, and a sense of calm.

Sports psychologists help Olympic athletes ensure better visualization of success by providing guided visualizations. Such a coach helps ensure that athletes spend 20 minutes or so relaxing first, before beginning mental practice, because they know that best results come from a place of peaceful, relaxed detachment before doing imagery rehearsal. Sports psychologists assist athletes in focusing on visualizing themselves doing better at particular physical activities they've been challenged with before, such as improving a golf swing.

Thanks to magnetic resonance imaging (MRI) scans, neuroscientists have begun to explain a mechanism to account for why imaginary practice can be so extraordinarily effective. Dr. Thomas Newmark explains,

> *"Internal visualization of specific movements creates neural patterns in the brain, improving neuromuscular coordination. Because the brain tells the muscles how to move, stronger neural patterns thus result in 'clearer, stronger movement.' Results are then reinforced by gains made in actual practice, where real muscle activity occurs."*

While magnetic resonance imaging (MRI) scans can help provide us with rational explanations for the way our muscles

89

respond during imaginary practice, they don't entirely account for all types of improvement athletes enjoy. For example, some visualization suggestions mysteriously appear to work despite there being no precise set of muscle groups the athlete can practice working together.

A couple of case study examples provided in Dr. Newmark's research include the effective suggestion that a golfer drive the ball with *"laser-like accuracy,"* and the beneficial intimation that a football player catch each pass as if *"glue keeps the ball stuck"* to his hands. Both of these visualizations were effective even though they did not correspond to an obvious set of muscular movements. Clearly there is something more going on than simply programming various muscle groups... something we haven't yet found a way to measure with modern day MRI technology, but that we can achieve through visualization.

Picture yourself moving through your new daily activities in your most desired life. Imagine your future self is reaching a hand out and back to help make it easier for you to think, feel, speak and behave more in accordance with the person you'd most like to become. Notice what is most noticeably different, and pay attention to how you can start behaving more like this possible future self. Even doing the simplest little actions in the direction of living true to your dreams makes a huge difference.

With each newfound pattern of thought, emotional response, speech, and physical action, you are making it easier for you to develop the most optimal behaviors and habits that best correspond with your new life.

Step Three: Take Positive Action

To experience positive, memorable, meaningful quantum jumps, you must maintain a lucid state of fearlessness and love, while taking positive action in keeping with the reality of your dreams. Your feeling of love must be genuine for best results, rather than merely doing what has to be done out of obligation, duty, or expectation. Taking some kind of positive action while feeling so much love is akin to having a good attitude in life: doing what needs to be done with a song in your heart and a skip in your step, rather than feeling disconnected or disheartened. When you are facing a situation in which you most desire to make a quantum jump, you probably won't initially be feeling anything close to the level of love you'll need to make the leap to a new reality with such a positive state of unified body, heart, and mind.

So how do you focus on love when you're not starting out feeling love, and fake or forced feelings don't count? Fortunately, it is possible through focusing awareness in prayer or meditation to nurture your feelings of love. You can jump-start good feelings of love by remembering, for example, how much you love a favorite pet, best friend, child, or sibling.

When you breathe deeply, slowly, and rhythmically while regaining a deep sense of loving connection to something or someone else, you are helping to naturally harmonize your breathing with your heartbeat with your blood pressure. Attaining such a healthy state of resonance reduces feelings of stress while increasing a general sense of peace and wellbeing.

Once you feel a strong sensation of love—that you might physically feel as warmth in your heart—you can focus your attention on the reality you are choosing for yourself and know what action you can now take that is in keeping with being the new you.

Imagine that this reality is also now choosing and coming toward you every bit as much as you are now choosing and coming to it, so you are now gaining insights and inspiration regarding what you can best think, say, and do.

Getting Started with Quantum Jumps

In truth, you've been quantum jumping without realizing that's what you've been doing for quite some time. The difference between quantum jumping when you know you're doing it consists of learning how to move out of current patterns of thoughts and behaviors to new ones that are associated with the reality you are jumping into.

One of the best ways to get a feel for quantum jumping is to recognize practical applications in matters of importance to you as they arise. Two common types of real-life problems quantum jumping is good at resolving include finding lost things and overcoming health problems.

Finding Lost Things Quantum Jumps

The following examples of finding lost things gives you an idea of what it can feel like to move from a state of feeling separated from an important object, and the surprise and joy of seeing it turn up, often quite unexpectedly.

I experienced a remarkable reality shift in which my friend's missing eyeglasses materialized after both of us had conducted a very thorough search of the house. My friend commented that his glasses were not anywhere they would be expected to be... not in pockets, or on a table, or a counter, or a chair. We retraced his steps around the house, and still didn't see them anywhere... including in his car or out on the street by the car. I asked my friend to describe his glasses to me, which helped me gain a clear impression of what his glasses looked like in their case.

I then felt how much I loved my friend, and how important these glasses were to him, as we walked once more around the house. In this state of walking meditation, I held a vision of what the glasses looked like, while feeling relaxed, confident, and loving. I knew that when things of importance go missing, there's no need to panic. In fact, I remembered that it's best to calm down, any time my friend or I started feeling worried.

I knew from first-hand experience that the best state of mind for having lost items reappear is to feel relaxed, yet excited that at some point the items will return. On the very next stroll through my kitchen, I heard a soft "thump" sound one pace behind where I'd just walked. I spun around to see what had made the noise, and saw I was the only one in the area... and there just a couple of feet from me, on the kitchen floor, were my friend's glasses!

Healing Quantum Jumps

Wisconsin organic homesteader, John Matzke, was thirty years old and a brand-new father in 1974 when doctors found a lump in his armpit. A biopsy of the lump confirmed the worst —malignant melanoma. The tumors were removed, but ten years later, in 1984, cancer spread to John's lungs. Dr. Joseph F. O'Donnell, John's oncologist at the Veteran's Administration hospital in White River Junction, Vermont, knew John's survival chances were slim and urged John to undergo immediate treatment. Dr. O'Donnell explained that once melanoma gains a foothold in an internal organ such as the lungs, the typical outcome is death, which usually comes in a matter of months without immediate treatment.... and even with treatment, John's chances looked slim; only 50% of all melanoma patients with lung metastases are alive 30 months after surgery.

Rather than follow Dr. O'Donnell's recommendation for immediate treatment, John took a month off to strengthen his body to prepare for the grueling ordeal of chemotherapy. John took long hikes in the fresh air of the mountains, ate healthy foods, meditated, and imagined himself healthy with good strong blood cells destroying cancer in his body. When John flew back to Vermont so Dr. O'Donnell could X-ray his chest and document the size and location of the tumor in his lung, they were both surprised. As Dr. O'Donnell remembers,

"When John came back a month later, it was remarkable —the tumor on his chest X-ray was gone. Gone, gone, gone."

Institute of Noetic Sciences researchers Brendan O'Regan and Caryle Hirshberg clarified the meaning of interchangeable terms *spontaneous regression* and *spontaneous remission* to be:

the disappearance, complete or incomplete, of a disease or cancer without medical treatment or treatment that is considered inadequate to produce the resulting disappearance of disease symptoms or tumor.

Evidence of Quantum Jumps through Parallel Worlds

Now that we know, or begin to suspect, that we are living in a Quantum Age of entanglement, superposition of states and teleportation... how might we recognize that we have, in fact, arrived in a parallel universe? While we won't get our multiverse passports stamped each time we make a journey to a parallel world, we can expect to see the occasional indication that the world we're in now is a bit different than worlds we've left behind. We'd expect to occasionally hear reports of abrupt and otherwise inexplicable changes being observed. Such reports could include hearing that someone we'd seen reported dead is alive again, or a place we've visited is now called something different and is decorated differently—yet people who work there claim it's always been this way, and have photos to prove it... yet we know what we saw. Or we might re-read a favorite book and notice it's not the same, or watch a movie again and find pivotal scenes are different now.

One of the best ways to gain an appreciation for just how often we're traveling between parallel worlds is to tell people or keep a journal of some of the ways we observe reality to be changing or shifting around us. We can read experiences of quantum jumps and reality shifts, and reality shifting survey results in order to recognize a wider variety of signs that indicate we might be traveling between worlds.

Survey Results Show Signs of Quantum Jumps

You might well be wondering that if quantum jumps are such a natural part of life, where is the evidence that such things are actually occurring? If people are observing signs of moving between parallel worlds, we'd expect to see some evidence of these kinds of quantum jumps from time to time. The RealityShifters website has conducted two reality shifting surveys with hundreds of survey participants over a span of thirteen years in order to determine exactly that. Specifically, these surveys were designed to track what types of shifts in reality people are noticing, and what changes, if any, are occurring in the types of reality shifts most commonly observed over time.

In April 2000, *"How Do You Shift Reality?"* survey of 395 people was conducted through the RealityShifters website. Respondents answered a series of questions about how often and whether they experienced such things as synchronicity, finding a parking place where and when they need one, and experiencing time seem to slow down, stop, or speed up. People were encouraged to participate regardless of whether they believed they'd ever experienced the phenomenon of reality shifts in their lives or not. Survey participants for the 2000 survey were contacted through the RealityShifters ezine, and subscribers were encouraged to invite friends, colleagues and family to complete surveys, too.

The *How Do You Shift Reality?"* survey was conducted again in May 2013 with 567 respondents. These respondents were contacted via social media (Facebook and Twitter) as well as through the RealityShifters ezine. A new question was added about noticing seeing people or animals alive again who'd previously been reported or observed to be dead. Answers received for the second survey were remarkably consistent with the first, within a few percentage points in most cases.

What stands out the most in these survey results is that a whopping majority of 93% of all respondents reported are currently noticing synchronicity and coincidence in their daily life; 90% report having seen time seem to slow down, stop, or speed up (up from 86% in 2000); and 83% report that they often find parking spaces where and when they need them most (up from 78% in 2000). This means that more than three quarters of the population is currently experiencing some pretty amazing phenomena!

The next most commonly reported type of reality shift was reported by 69% of those surveyed: sometimes putting things down in one place (such as keys, wallet or coat) only to find them missing or moved later on. 57% of respondents reported occasionally seeing things jump, leap, or fall without anyone moving them; 44% of respondents observed things transforming into something different than they'd been before, and 48% of respondents reported having seen people, plants, animals or things appear out of thin air (up from 45% in 2000). 35% of respondents reported having seen business signs inexplicably changing their hours; 33% reported having seen people, plants, animals and things disappear; 22% reported seeing doors lock or unlock by themselves; and 15% of respondents reported having seen objects transport or teleport themselves miles away from their points of origination (exactly the same percentage in both surveys).

One of the *How Do You Shift Reality?"* survey questions asked people how they felt when they had experienced reality shifts in which something appeared, disappeared, transported or transformed, or there was some change to the experience of time. The most common reaction reported by 30% of those surveyed was that they felt curious about reality shifts when these things happened. Curiosity was followed by feeling awestruck (18%), excited (17%), happy (16%) and confused (10%). Only 1% of respondents felt frightened, only four survey respondents (0%) felt angry, and not even one single person reported ever feeling sad when observing reality shifts.

2000	2013	Survey Question:
95%	93%	Notice synchronicity & coincidences
78%	83%	Find parking places where needed
72%	69%	Witness things going missing
54%	62%	See people & animals heal after prayer
86%	90%	Time slows down, stops & speeds up
55%	57%	Things move without being touched
37%	35%	Business hours change
21%	22%	Doors lock or unlock by themselves
51%	44%	Things have been transformed
8%	10%	Bent spoons, keys, coins or other
45%	48%	Seen people, animals, things appear
18%	15%	Seen objects travel distances or teleport
33%	33%	Seen people, plants, animals disappear
(N.A.)	27%	Seen dead people, animals alive again
21%	14%	Notice reality shifts daily
22%	23%	Notice reality shifts weekly
21%	21%	Notice reality shifts monthly
5%	8%	Notice reality shifts annually
22%	25%	Notice reality shifts very rarely
6%	7%	Don't notice reality shifts at all

The chart on the opposite page shows the survey questions asked in the 2000 and 2013 surveys, together with the percentage of people reporting they have experienced each type of reality shift. Some of the questions have to do with the frequency that people notice reality shifts (daily, weekly, monthly, annually, very rarely, or not at all).

27% of those surveyed in 2013 responded "Yes" to the new question, "Have you seen dead people, plants or animals alive again?" indicating these things are observed just slightly less often than seeing people, plants, animals or things disappear.

In the write-in section for comments, some people expressed having a need to rationalize what just happened, or that they felt: dumbfounded, awestruck, humbled, grateful, a heightened sense of awareness, and feeling very alive. Others expressed indifference, mystification, or ambivalence. Here are some write-in comments from the survey:

"Yee-haw!"

"As Spock would say, 'Interesting!'"

"Just glad to be able to see it and feel it when it happens"

"These are natural occurrences for me and I'm not alarmed."

"Sometimes I feel ambivalent—as if 'of course,' no big deal."

"I try to hold on to the moment as long as possible."

"I suddenly feel small in the scheme of things."

"I've experienced them with witnesses but don't know if they noticed."

Reality shifts can feel most enjoyable when you're not the only one noticing them. Having someone else present to validate that you're remembering things correctly feels priceless when something's just changed and you're likely starting to doubt your memory. While 41% of those surveyed said they've only witnessed reality shifts while alone, 28% have shared the experience with another person, 11% have been with two other witnesses, 2% have had three others present, and 3% have had more than ten other witnesses to the experience.

Quantum Jumps to Change the Past

We shift between parallel possible worlds with every choice we make. Since most of our choices are subconscious (sitting up straight, scratching, whether or not we smile as someone enters the room), we are seldom aware that we've just jumped to another reality, let alone that we just changed both our possible futures and our possible pasts. When we change the way we perceive events in our lives, we have the power to change the past.

While you may not think you've ever changed the past, you've likely done so every time you've become grateful for people, experiences, events or things you hadn't previously fully appreciated. Gratitude is a lot like looking in the rear view mirror of life, and instead of just seeing storm clouds and miles of bad road, seeing the beauty of rainbows. A number of studies have shown that keeping a gratitude journal or finding some other way to practice gratitude on a regular basis helps people in a number of ways, including: better health, sounder sleep, reduced anxiety and depression, and greater happiness. One of the best ways to utilize a gratitude journal is to make a daily list of what you're most thankful for, and take a moment to also mention what you've had to do with bringing these things into being. Simply making the connection between yourself and what you most appreciate can be enough to lift you out of depressive funks, to a new image of yourself as being a positive force for good in the world.

The value of changing the past becomes abundantly clear whenever we need healing from illness or injury. For those who've witnessed instantaneous remission of cancer, healing of broken bones, bruises, burns or cuts—such healing feels like moving to another reality. The new reality is one in which the previous sequence of events does not play out quite the same way, thank goodness! While all of us are capable of intentionally changing the past, this particular skill is something that some meditation masters, lucid dreamers, and near death experiencers truly excel at, with their awareness of being pure consciousness.

What I've learned about changing the past is that best results are possible when we emotionally detach to an inner place of peacefulness that is non-judgmental and full of love. It is challenging to influence past events when we are charged up with strong feelings, since emotions are like gears that engage and lock in certain realities. To get to a past you enjoy better, you need to first change the way you feel all the way down to your subconscious gut feelings. Through meditation or lucid dreaming, you can envision first being pure energy—pure consciousness—existing between realities, where all possibilities can be seen. This detachment allows you to change your habitual emotional patterns from fear to love and gratitude.

When setting out to change the past, don't focus overly much on your goal of changing the past, because ironically, for most people, that only serves to fix the past event more rigidly in place. Instead, focus on what you love most that is happening now, has happened in the past, and that you treasure most dearly. Relaxing in an energized state is the key to success, with detachment from any expectations of what should be, or should have been, could be or could have been, or would be or would have been. When you omit dwelling on the shoulda-coulda-woulda's of life, and focus your attention on everything that opens your heart up so wide it feels like it's going to burst, you're in a much better quantum jumping state of mind.

Lucid Dreaming

> *"Only by increasing our conscious awareness in the dream state can we ever realize the nature of the reality we experience."*
>
> — *Robert Waggoner*

Lucid dreaming is a tool you can learn to master that helps you succeed with quantum jumping by knowing you are awake within the dream. Dreams provide gateways to the portals by which we select realities, and neuroscientists are discovering that lucid dreamers have an advantage when it comes to learning new things. Most people are limited more by what they think their limitations are, just as most people are limited by their dreams when they accept dream situations as being all that is possible. By learning to awaken within their dreams, lucid dreamers enjoy a means by which they can most fully and vibrantly explore new experiences and ways of being... trying out many creative possibilities one at a time, to see where each one goes. When we explore reality selection via lucid dreams, we activate an awareness of reality that exists outside any particular given space-time or possible reality, so our dream explorations are able to take us further than our imagination alone usually does.

Dreams can be quite real... in fact, sometimes dreams can feel realer than real. Yet when we learn to awaken within our dreams and recognize that we are, in fact, dreaming, this newfound lucidity can help us recognize the very process by which we select realities. Lucid dreamers recognize coming in contact with a consciousness bigger than they are when engaged in lucid dreams, and this larger sense of consciousness can interact with lucid dreamers in surprising, unexpected ways. For example, some lucid dreamers find they are suddenly aware of intimate details from other peoples' lives who they've had no prior direct contact or exchange of information with. Sometimes this information might be of direct significance for the lucid dreamer's life, and other times it might be meaningful to others.

Robert Waggoner is president-elect of the International Association for the Study of Dreams (IASD), and editor of the Lucid Dream Exchange. Waggoner describes the startling accuracy of one man's lucid dreams with regard to a woman's deceased husband. Ed dreamed of the woman's dead husband in a lucid dream that turned out to be simply packed full of information that was not consciously known to Ed at the time. In the lucid dream, Ed dreamt of being with the man in a dimly lit dream environment of metal walls and metal doors with no windows—which he later found out was very similar to the type of submarines his friend's dead husband had fond memories of working on while serving in the Navy. Ed also dreamt of an old dictation machine, which he later discovered was amongst the man's most cherished possessions. In Ed's lucid dream, the deceased man talked about the wonder of calligraphy, which was indeed one of the deceased's favorite hobbies while alive.

Daniel Erlacher has proven in research studies conducted at the University of Bern, Switzerland, that lucid dreamers who practice throwing a coin into a cup improve their subsequent performance at that task by 8%—much better than non-lucid dreamers and those who made no attempt to practice in their dreams, though not as much as the experimental subjects who

103

practice in waking life. In another experiment, Erlacher noted that people asked to practice deep knee bends in their sleep had elevated heart and respiratory rates while dreaming, as if they were actually exercising.

Yale University Associate Professor Dr. Peter Thomas Morgan has received a $3 million research grant to fund studies on the way alcohol and cocaine affect peoples' brains, and a relatively meager $15,000 for his research into what is going on when people experience lucid dreams... yet lucid dream studies are near and dear to Morgan's heart. Morgan's interest in lucid dreaming began when he was a teenager in Livermore, California and first becoming interested in medicine. Within weeks of hearing a radio program about how to have lucid dreams, Morgan felt exhilarated to be dreaming lucidly. Morgan explains what he loves about lucid dreaming:

> "Sleep sometimes can be scary. It's giving up to the darkness, to the nothingness. For a lucid dreamer, you're not doing that. You're just going into another sate where you're still going to be there."

Around this same time, Morgan was involved in a skiing accident, where he briefly lost consciousness. He recalls,

> "It felt just like a jump in my timeline from being upright, getting the sense that I might be falling, to being 10 or 20 feet down the hill, spinning around and going down quickly on my back and tumbling. Something about the experience didn't accrue whatever was required to have that sort of remembered present, so it got me philosophizing about consciousness."

The remarkable thing to Morgan about this experience was how he momentarily lost a sense of meta-awareness—awareness of being aware.

With the help of high school student Michelle Neider, Morgan conducted a weeklong study at Michelle's Briarcliff High School to see whether the brains of lucid dreamers functioned differently than brains of non-lucid dreamers. Morgan's hypothesis was that lucid-dreaming students would tend to perform better on cognitive tasks that engage the ventromedial prefrontal cortex (such as the Iowa Gambling Task in which participants are asked to select cards from one of four decks in order to gain as much virtual money as possible), but would perform the same as their peers on tasks that engage the dorsolateral prefrontal cortex (such as the Wisconsin Card Sort Task in which participants are asked to sort cards based on color or shape with no guidance on how to sort them)... and Morgan's hypothesis proved to be true. Lucid dreamers, even while wide awake, are fundamentally different from non-lucid dreamers with regard to activities where emotions play a role in decision-making.

Frequent lucid dreamers, such as Robert Waggoner, describe accessing a dream state in which they know they are dreaming, often because something unusual has caught their attention inside the dream. Such tip-offs might include seeing someone they know to be dead or far away, or inexplicably rapid changes in peoples' hair or clothes. Once awake within the dream, it's then possible to ask questions either aloud or by thinking them, and observe answers coming in any of a number of different ways. Dream realities bring together people, places and things through a wide variety of times, intermingling events in nonlinear fashion.

Given that the true nature of reality is quite possibly that time is actually nonlinear, such interconnectedness in our dreaming states provides us with access to a wide number of possible realities. When people develop lucid dreaming abilities, they often notice an increase in synchronicity and other forms of reality shifts, alternate histories, and evidence of having made quantum jumps.

Receive Help from a Positive Future

"If you want to understand what is happening at any point in time, it's not just the past that is relevant. It's also the future."
— *Jeff Tollaksen*

Just as University of Washington physicist John Cramer proposes a transactional interpretation of quantum mechanics, we can imagine a synchronizing effect occurring between our most desired futures and this present time. We typically consider the past to be fixed and the future unknown and open to change... yet what if both future and past are free to move? We can expect to receive occasional inspiration and assistance in the form of daydreams, visions, and dreams.

Author PMH Atwater describes viewing glimpses into her future that she saw in 1978 while living in Boise, Idaho. These glimpses came to her as "a field of brilliant sparkles" that surrounded her, in which she saw herself getting a job in Washington, D.C., and later moving to the state of Virginia. She saw herself visiting many places she'd long dreamed of along the way, and eventually ending up with a man she would love, marry, and have children with.

The idea of bicausality in physics is an elegant and mathematically correct stance by which to consider ourselves moving through space and time. In our ordinary experience of time, we move forward through time, and observe entropy as decision trees branch into greater complexity from the past to the future. By envisioning a balance between the diverging forward-time movement of causality and the converging reverse-time movement of retrocausality, we are able to gain a sense of a supercausal state of being in which past, present and future coexist together.

Life itself appears to be sustained by syntropy and the organizing balance between forward and reverse causality. A growing number of scientific studies supports this hypothesis, showing how our autonomic nervous system consistently responds prior to receiving physical signals from environmental stimuli. Experiencing such a supercausal state of being thus feels like we are creating in both the future and the past, dancing between alternate realities and taking turns between being members of an appreciative audience and inspired storytellers.

By envisioning ourselves as participants in this dance, it's clear that there is some part of ourselves we can imagine—our best possible future selves—who already know the optimal solution for us and everyone and everything we love. Much in the way that plants so efficiently choose just the best path for photosynthesis, knowing that some part of ourselves has already seen and tried out all possible paths in our lives can provide us with a focus for helping ensure greater health, prosperity and success in our lives. In this way, we can expect to get glimpses of our best possible futures, and can stay open to receiving such inspiration.

All the exercises at the end of this chapter are designed to help you experience the most enjoyable quantum jumps, and one of them shows you how you can receive help from your best possible future self on a daily basis. Just as there are many facets to your personality, and you're much more than any of the many roles in life you've played so far, so too is your best possible future self. Imagine all the aspects of people you most admire— the qualities you appreciate most in your favorite people in the world. These qualities can be yours, with an accompanying whole new wonderful way of life to go with it.

Be careful to include everything you *truly* most value and cherish, rather than simply focusing on qualities you *think* you should care most about. This helps you avoid ending up becoming someone you wouldn't really like. In the movie, *The Kid*, a man named Russ played by actor Bruce Willis meets a younger version of himself, Rusty, who is thoroughly unimpressed upon seeing his future self. *"So I'm forty, I'm not married, I don't fly jets, and I don't have a dog? I grow up to be a loser."* This poignant line of movie dialogue touches a nerve in every one of us who loves to laugh and play, and deep down isn't fooled into thinking that everything advertised is something we must have.

When we're open to receiving guidance from our very best possible future selves, we can sometimes get the feeling we're looking at the answer to a problem in the back of the book. This kind of future memory visualization from all possible future paths helps us know which direction will prove to be optimal for us. This kind of inspiration helps us remain true to our core principles, while having fun, feeling inspired, and gaining confidence that life just keeps getting better and better all the time!

*   *   *

Would you like to read about successful quantum jumps people have enjoyed? Chapter Four's *Quantum Jump Experiences* is designed to give you lots of good quantum jumping ideas and inspiration from real-life examples of quantum jumps!

Exercise

Believe It's Already Yours

Close your eyes and imagine you're looking at a dial—
like a fuel gauge on your car—that shows the current
reading of Desire versus Belief that what you're seeking
is already yours. Just like a fuel gauge shows 'empty' on
one side and 'full' on the other, imagine this dial
moving from where it is now all the way to 'Belief.'
Imagine what it feels like to be filled with gratitude that
the specific quality, experience, or thing you'd most love
in your life is already yours. Savor that feeling of
thankfulness... and see how far that dial has moved
from 'desire' to 'belief.'

Exercise

Feel Gratitude for Everything

Close your eyes, breathe slowly and deeply, and feel
yourself relaxing all your muscles, starting with your feet
and legs feeling comfortably warm and heavy, and
moving up through your entire body. Think of someone
or something wonderful from your past that is a truly
happy memory, and take several moments to appreciate
how thankful you are for that special time.

While still taking slow and deep breaths, gradually
expand your awareness to other events and people in
your life, observing your life as one would watch a
movie on a movie screen, with you starring as the lead
character in your life story. Feel gratitude for all the
supporting events and characters and people in your
life, and breathe deeply and fully as you allow these
feelings of appreciation to flow through and around
you.

Exercise

Heaven on Earth

Imagine experiencing a feeling of oneness and perfect harmony. Allow yourself to relax and enjoy feeling a complete sense of love, joy, peace, and balance... knowing you are perfectly safe, happy, and well. From this vantage point, realize you have access to all realms of possibility, and can watch possible scenes from your future stretch out before you. You may see scenes from your future in which you are happily doing things you've longed to do but not yet felt capable or confident doing... or you might see scenes from your future in which you master ways to be of service to others beyond anything you've previously envisioned. Hold whatever vision you see that you find most appealing in mind, while breathing fully and deeply, and feeling as positively emotionally energized as possible.

Exercise

Guided by Your Best Possible Future Self

Place one hand over your heart center, more toward the middle of your chest than your physical heart, and close your eyes as you breathe deep, full breaths. Envision that your best possible future self is here with you now, providing you with inspiration to make the best possible choices in your life from this moment on. Imagine how your newfound advantage of guidance and support from your best possible future self will make your life better every day in every possible way. Envision your best possible future self, as you imagine yourself being guided forward effortlessly and easily to be in the right place at the right time—doing, thinking, and saying the right things.

Exercise

Lucid Dreaming

You can prompt lucid dreams by knowing you can wake up within a dream and know you're dreaming. Before you go to sleep, tell yourself that you're going to wake up in one your dreams tonight. Think of something you can do inside the dream when you realize, "I'm dreaming!" to confirm you really are awake within the dream. You might look at your hands, for example, or clasp your hands together in a certain way while looking at them. Keep a journal near where you sleep, so when you awaken you can write down any dreams you remember—lucid or not—when you awaken.

Exercise

Experience Being Pure Consciousness

The goal of this meditation is to disengage from viewing yourself in terms of physical, material qualities, in order that you can experience yourself as existing in the form of pure consciousness. Start by closing your eyes and observing whatever thoughts and feelings you experience. Rather than thinking you are the one thinking these thoughts or having these feelings, realize that you are the one observing a human who is having such thoughts and feelings. Recognize that you are not your thoughts, and you are not your feelings. Say to yourself, *"I am the one who observes a human having thoughts and feelings."* Imagine in this state of awareness that all possible realities are now accessible to you, and you can see where the results of each choice and each decision lead. Realize that in this state of being pure consciousness, the most enjoyable and best realities present themselves to you easily and effortlessly.

"Truth is stranger than fiction,
but it is because Fiction
is obliged to stick to possibilities;
Truth isn't."
— *Mark Twain*

Chapter 4

Quantum Jump

Experiences

Imagine dancing through a multiverse in which you're moving forward through space-time with one hand outstretched before you in a handshake with the future, and your other hand reaching back to a point in your past. As you move through this pattern in a large circular square dance, you're dancing what's called a "grand right and left" pattern, with half the dancers moving clockwise in the time-forward (retarded) motion we're accustomed to, and the other half moving in counter-clockwise time-backward (advanced) direction. We can think of this cosmic bi-causal folk dance as representing an exchange of information between our future and our present, and our present and our past. At each decision point where we choose whose hand we hold with a partner going the opposite direction, we have the opportunity to obtain information about what's ahead of or behind us—in the form of intuitive hunches and premonitions.

One such premonitory insight was received on Monday, the 7th of May 1979, by a Manchester mother named Kate. She'd planned to go into town on Tuesday with her daughter to purchase two Lego Thatcher Perkins trains—one for herself and another for a friend in Wales—because she'd heard these toys had been greatly reduced and were on sale at Woolworth's. Kate was taking advantage of the sunny day on Monday to do her laundry, when she was surprised to hear her Grandmother's voice, who'd died in 1956, telling her, "Go to town today." Kate says, "I said out loud, 'No, it might rain tomorrow,' and I heard her again, louder, insisting I go that day." Heeding the advice of this urgent message, Kate took her daughter shopping at the Woolworth's opposite Piccadilly Gardens, in what was at that time the largest Woolworth's in Europe, on the exact floor where a fire started the very next day. Kate heard about the terrible fire in which ten people died and 47 people were hospitalized on Tuesday, when her friend from Wales called to find out if she was OK, since he knew she'd planned to buy his train set there that day.

Many people who've enjoyed some of the most amazing quantum jumps have moved from an existence that felt confining, restrictive, and in some cases like it was coming to a close. Perhaps such life circumstances hold special opportunities for us, as we are more willing to let go of old beliefs and try something new when we feel we've hit a dead end.

Sometimes, quantum jumps occur just when we'd most wish them to, and other times they occur most unexpectedly, though it's likely true that in all cases there had been a long-standing desire to make a change. The key factor is often one of imagination—of allowing one's mind to wander to hitherto unknown realms, envisioning a new possible future very different from anything one's known before—yet one that beckons so invitingly that nothing else feels quite so compelling.

One of the best ways to get inspired to make quantum jumps in your life is to read actual experiences people have had with them. As you read through the following real-life accounts

114

of quantum jump experiences, ask yourself what kind of quantum jump experiences you'd most enjoy.

Pub Name and Colors Change

Linda from Loughton, Essex in England describes an extraordinary experience she had one day when walking her dog in a woodland conservation area. While sitting on a bench to rest, Linda was startled to note that a pub with brightly colored red doors and window frames was situated so close to the conservation area, in a spot one would expect businesses would be required to choose color palettes that blend in, rather than stand out. Linda made a mental note of the name of the pub, and a few weeks later when a friend came to visit, took the opportunity to return.

Linda noted with surprise when she got there that the pub was not painted red and white, but dark green and white. Linda assumed they'd been made to repaint, and also noted that the pub's name and sign had been changed. These changes hardly seemed to be an improvement, so when buying drinks at the bar, she made a point to ask the owner why they'd changed the name of the pub. He looked puzzled and said, "This pub has had the same name for 350 years!" He gestured to old drawings, paintings, and photographs in frames along the walls, showing the pub through the years, always with this name... and added it had never been red and white, either.

Linda was totally dumbfounded, and just sat for at least five minutes on the bench, looking at what was definitely the same pub... yet with different name, color, and signage. As Linda looked back on this experience and shared it with me, she felt that surely the first explanation that comes to mind when seeing such a change in reality is that you've shifted from one universe to a slightly different one.

115

Missing Engagement Ring Returned

At a time when Pam and her husband were going through some rocky times in their marriage, Pam was a self-described cynic with regard to paranormal activity of any kind. One evening while she was washing her wedding and engagement rings at the kitchen sink in her home in Bloomington, Illinois, Pam's engagement ring slipped out of her fingers... and disappeared. It made no sound when it fell, so she didn't know where it had gone, and so she searched everywhere—including the floor, the sink, and the counter. Pam ran out of time to search that evening, as she and her husband were expected at a formal function, but Pam made sure to ask her husband if he'd please take the sink apart so she could resume her search first thing in the morning. Upon returning home from her night with friends, Pam changed out of her evening clothes and spent another 45 minutes looking for her missing ring unsuccessfully.

The next morning, Pam got up early and used a flashlight to inspect the drain, the faucet, and every nook and cranny within 20 feet of the sink. Pam then awakened her husband, who came to inspect every area Pam had already covered, confirming there was no sign of it. He took apart the pipes, but found no ring. Pam looked down into the sink again from above, while he jiggled the pipes. He put the pipes back together and asked Pam to start the water, so he could check the seal. Pam went to turn on the water, and screamed a cry of astonishment. There was Pam's ring, sitting in the flat, clear bottom of the sink—bone-dry with no water or pipe 'gook' on it. Pam and her husband got the chills, and stood transfixed for minutes, trying to explain the whole thing to one another—trying to come up with some 'normal' explanation of how the ring could be missing and then just be there. To this day, Pam and her husband still get chills when thinking about this experience, and happily they made it through their rocky times, and are still together, best of friends, and deeply thankful for their marriage.

Finding Missing Jewelry Box in New Place

Missing things can be found quite a bit later than they initially vanish, as I discovered when I found my miniature travel jewelry box was missing from my purse. I felt terrible shock when I first discovered it was not in my purse, to the point I was feeling almost faint. This small jewelry box had been holding some of my very favorite jewelry that was precious to me both for its monetary value and for sentimental reasons. Some of the earrings had been hand-made by a dear friend, and were irreplaceable.

The first thought that occurred to me when I emptied my purse out and confirmed it wasn't there was that someone had either taken the jewelry box, or it had fallen out of my purse at some point while I was out of town. Both possibilities were upsetting, and left me feeling more agitated. I immediately calmed myself down, reminding myself that I know from past experiences that fretting usually only ever leads to further misfortune. Instead of worrying, I imagined that my beloved jewelry box was on its way back to me, somehow. I searched my purse many more times, and started getting a feeling that my jewelry box might show up in a new place—somewhere it had never been before. Specifically, I started getting a feeling that it might show up in a completely new place that I'd never kept it before, such as in one of my dresser drawers.

Each day for at least ten days, I would go through another iteration of this process, starting with a jolt of panic and alarm that reminded me to calm myself down. Specifically, I'd calm myself down with a happy thought that my jewelry box was definitely coming back to me. After many days of doing this,

117

some time in the second week of it's absence, I was astonished to reach into one of my dresser drawers and find my jewelry box right on top, with all contents intact. I was thrilled and amazed!

Healed by a New Name

Once we understand the tremendous power of placebos, we're more likely to seriously contemplate how in traditional Chinese society, name doctors exist who assist with renaming babies suffering from chronic illness. The idea behind these name changes is that there is some kind of mismatch between child and name—which is something that when corrected through renaming, releases the sickness associated with the child with the previous name. This practice was reported by authors Gary Lee and Nicholas Tapp in their study of the Hmong, and is still going strong in the last couple of decades, as reported by my daughter whose Chinese friend was renamed while sick as an infant some twenty years ago. Babies aren't the only ones to receive renaming assistance; people may be renamed at any traumatic point in life where they can benefit from a fresh infusion of inspiration and positive energy.

Quantum jumps occur much more frequently than most people realize, and some of the most inspirational quantum jumps have provided people tremendous boosts in health, wealth, or skills they'd not previously enjoyed. Not only can quantum jumps provide us with entirely new skills and abilities, they can also transport people to new vistas, landscapes, and worlds.

Quantum Jump Out of 24-Hour Flu

A woman named Julia from Evanston, Illinois shared her healing experience with me for my RealityShifters ezine, describing to me how she recovered from a 24-hour flu virus that was simply horrendous. As Julia described it, "This was a horrible flu—I had seen my husband and son go through twenty four hours of, well, you know—leakage—from all body parts that can leak." In the first half hour of coming down with this dreadful flu, Julia remembered the concept of reality shifts while gazing at a picture that she saw slowly disappearing. She was feverish, about to pass out, and losing water very fast as she sat in the bathroom at the beginning of an ordeal she 'knew' would last all day. As she remembered the concept of reality shifts—of how we can change instantaneously, she said to herself, "Now I will see the whole picture; now I will have no fever; now I will be re-energized; and now all symptoms will stop."

Julia remembers thinking to herself, *"If reality shifts are real, then one can happen right now. I dare you, flu, to go away."* Everyone who's done something similar knows what happened next. Julia didn't pass out, her vision cleared, her fever vanished and all symptoms cleared, much to the amazement of her family.

Reduced Blood Pressure by Thinking of Wonderful Time

Author and film director Raúl daSilva had an extraordinary, empowering reading by a full trance medium whose channeling confirmed many positive things and left Raúl feeling fulfilled, as he remembered spiritual lessons.

The morning after the reading, Raúl conducted an experiment while taking his blood pressure. Ordinarily, Raul's blood pressure tended to be a little on the high side, even with medication. He took an initial reading, and then visualized a time in his life when he was a 21-year-old freshman in college and Navy veteran. This was a point in Raúl's life when the world

119

held nothing but promise, and he'd not yet experienced traumas of the adult world. Raúl remembered a specific crystal-clear sunlit day at New York's Jones Beach from a time when he'd been working there as part of the New York State Park Police, informally known as "Parkway Police" since they patrolled Long Island highways that are known as parkways. On this beautiful day, all seemed perfect with the world. As Raul thought back to that pleasant time, he could even hear the surf breaking softly as seagulls called out in the distance.

After Raúl took his blood pressure reading again, he noticed it had dropped down by a full ten points! He tried envisioning that wonderful time in his past again, and noticed his blood pressure was now down where it was when he'd been 21 and felt at peace with the world! At that point in life, he'd been filled with bright, shining hope and the sun-filled, blue horizon ahead. With such clear confirmation from his blood pressure readings, Raúl realized he can always revisit that wonderful moment, and it can be a healing practice. As Raúl says, "We can all do it."

Finding True Love in a Telepathy Experiment

When Julie Beischel signed up to participate in a telepathy experiment, the last thing she expected was to fall in love. Beischel was in a room by herself, unable to see her experimental partner, Mark Boccuzzi. Boccuzzi's instructions were simply to gaze at Julie intently on a closed circuit screen that intermittently showed her (live) image. Intriguingly, the data showed Julie's physiological responses every time Mark could see her, with noticeable spikes at the exact moments her image was taken away—as if her body was saying, "Oh, where did he go?" Julie said. At the time, Julie didn't immediately tell Mark about the powerful connections she'd felt to him, since after all, they were strangers. Now married, Julie and Mark credit telepathy for helping them meet and fall in love. *"It was like nothing I had ever encountered,"* Julie said.

Finding True Love in a Dream

Late in the middle of a cold November night, Bette went back to sleep after the police had run her abusive alcoholic husband off from the premises for what felt like the millionth time. Bette climbed into bed next to her eleven-year-old daughter who'd fallen asleep by her side, watching the 10 o'clock news. Seeing it was now 2 AM, Bette closed her eyes, thinking about responsibilities at her new job and how the billing cycles worked.

Bette heard the voice of her supervisor, and woke up with a start at 4 AM to see him standing beside her bed. She started to speak, but felt his hand reach out to gently touch her mouth as he shook his head, "no." With his mouth closed, Bette heard him say, "Come," and hand-in-hand they walked through a wooded grove to a waterfall. Bette felt a closeness and loving connection with him unlike anything she'd ever before experienced, and stepped together with him into the waterfall. They held hands and walked back to her bedroom, where Bette looked at the clock to see it was 6:30 am.

Fully awake now, Bette was stunned to see her hair was wet, and she went to the kitchen to get a drink. As Bette stood at the sink, she felt arms around her body and the familiar voice softly saying, *"I love you. I will always love and take care of you,"* in her ear. Bette could even smell his scent... and then he was gone.

Upon returning to work, the first person Bette saw was her supervisor, who with eyes widened made a point of walking away without a word—avoiding her. A few days later, Bette's supervisor mentioned on a break, *"I had a dream about you,"* and

Bette told him she'd dreamed of him, too. He said, *"So it was real,"* and Bette replied, *"Yes it was."* He asked Bette to marry him, and she happily accepted. They've celebrated November 7th as their true anniversary ever since their shared dream of love became a dream-come-true.

There's Always Room for One More Good One

In 1956 when Leonard Nimoy was just out of the Army and living in Los Angeles with his wife and first child, he took a job as a taxi driver. He'd been away from doing any kind of acting for a few years, and had established very little in the way of a body of acting work to build upon, having mostly done a few uncredited roles.

When Mr. Nimoy picked up a Mr. Kennedy from a Bel-Air hotel, he recognized this was Senator Jack Kennedy. This was a time before Kennedy had attained national prominence, but Nimoy recognized Jack from having been born and raised in Boston. Nimoy struck up a conversation with Senator Kennedy, explaining that he was interested to hear from someone in his home state of Massachusetts.

Kennedy asked what Nimoy was doing in Los Angeles, and Nimoy replied that he was a hopeful actor. During this conversation, Senator Kennedy offered Nimoy some advice that stayed with him for the rest of his life, profoundly affecting him with inspirational words we can all benefit from should we choose to take them to heart:

"Your business is the same as mine.
There's a lot of competition.
But keep in mind, there's always room
for one more good one."

College Pennants on the Wall

Academy-Award winning actor Denzel Washington recalls that while growing up in Mount Vernon, New York, his parents were so busy working several jobs that no one was home to greet him most days after school. Thanks to the Boys Club, young Denzel was fortunate to have a strong role model in his life who encouraged him to think and dream big, despite being an inner city kid some might have labeled "troubled youth"—caught between school and the streets. At this place and time, few kids from Mount Vernon headed for college, but Billy Thomas had a brilliant idea. Billy expected each young man who graduated from high school and went away to college to send him the college pennant from their school. Billy then hung these college pennants on the Boys Club wall for all the boys to see.

Denzel recalls looking up at the college pennants hanging so proudly on the wall, each from a different city, a different college. Many of these were names and places he'd never heard of. With awe at the realization that some of the boys from his Boys Club were now going to school at these universities, Denzel thought to himself, *"Man, anything is possible!"* One of the pennants in particular captured Denzel's imagination—a pennant from USC. Denzel knew whose pennant it was; it came from Gus Williams, who was a couple of years ahead of Denzel and who was attending USC on a basketball scholarship. This particular pennant so completely captured Denzel's attention that he stared at it for hours.

> *"I'd never been anywhere outside Mount Vernon, but I just stared at that pennant and thought, 'OK, this guy I know, this guy I grew up with, he's out in California right now on a scholarship. He made it.' And then I thought, 'You know, if Gus can make it, then I can make it too.'"*

Setting an Example of Acting Like a Winner

The day women's basketball coach Kathy Delaney-Smith led her sixteenth-ranked Harvard team to victory playing Stanford University's top-ranked team marked one of the most amazing upsets in N.C.A.A. history. No Ivy League women's team had ever won a game in any N.C.A.A. tournament, let alone beat the strongest team in the nation. The secret behind Kathy Delaney-Smith's coaching boils down to one very simple philosophy: act as if you already are what you want to become.

"Act as if you're a great shooter," Delaney-Smith would instruct. *"Act as if you love the drill. Act as if when you hit the deck it doesn't hurt."* Zero tolerance for any form of negativity gave the Harvard women's basketball team a special kind of

advantage against teams with players who were clearly faster and stronger in many ways.

While such a Pollyanna attitude might come off sounding half-hearted from anyone who didn't truly walk their positivity talk, Delaney-Smith was the living embodiment of a self-made woman who built the foundation of her life on positive beliefs. Delaney-Smith originally became a basketball coach in 1969 as a favor to a friend, without ever having played competitive basketball. She made up for her lack of on-court experience by faking it the best she could, reading books and figuring out drills as she ran them. In addition to grueling physical training for her players, Kathy also led regular guided meditation sessions after practice, in which team members visualized bigger, stronger competitors in hostile away games.

Kathy's mind-body-spirit positivity made all the difference when she learned during a routine health exam in December 1999 that she'd been diagnosed with stage-two breast cancer. The tumor was larger than two centimeters, but had not yet spread through her body, and the lump was removed within a few weeks of its discovery. While undergoing chemotherapy, Delaney-Smith kept her sense of humor, and envisioned herself being well. Rather than hiding her condition from the basketball team, Delaney-Smith proactively had her hair cut short before it fell out.

Delaney-Smith recommends her athletes stay in the present moment, rather than worrying or fretting, saying, *"I stay in the moment pretty well. I think that's why I have less fear than many who get the disease."* Fourteen years after her cancer diagnosis, Delaney-Smith is still leading the Harvard women's basketball team to victory, and inspiring everyone who meets her to bring their best game to life, every single day.

Perfect Test Score While Asleep

An art teacher named Cathey described how one of the best and most amazing experiences she'd ever experienced had happened one summer when she was taking a final for a class. Cathey's life was so busy, with being the mother of five daughters, working, and attending graduate school that when the time came to take this particular final exam, she was feeling very tired and knew she had to close her eyes. She was sitting in the second row, directly in front of the professor in a full class of 30 students as she shut her eyes for a few seconds. When Cathey opened her eyes, she was amazed to see she'd completed the test! She checked her watch and saw she'd been 'asleep' for forty minutes. Not only were all 60 multiple choice questions answered, but the ten short essay questions were completed in her hand-writing as well!

Feeling very concerned about doing a good job on this important test, Cathey reviewed all her answers, and was glad to see they were all great and she didn't need to change any of them. Cathey'd once read that all knowledge from all of our possible realities exists and is available to us, if we can learn how to access it. She felt her relaxed state allowed her shift to a space where she could access what she already knew.

The thing that amazed Cathey most of all was that when she received her grade a week later, she found out she had a perfect score of 100 on this test! This was remarkably unusual, since while she usually earned good grades, she'd never before gotten 100% of the questions correct on any graduate level test.

Perfect Test Score While Feverishly Sick

I once earned a perfect score of 100% while taking a Statistics test in graduate school. I'd been sick with a fever but didn't want to miss this test, so I'd given myself a pep talk that
126

all I needed to do was get to the test on time, and do my best, and then I'd just go back home to bed. I had no test anxiety whatsoever for a change, as my whole world seemed collapsed in around my desk, my copy of the examination, and my pencil. Because thinking took such effort, I easily ignored any distractions from other students, or any stray thoughts. I was completely focused on just taking this test. I worked at a steady pace, with some kind of relaxed tunnel-vision of focus the whole time, turned my test in to my professor, and went home and straight back to bed.

When I got my test results, the teacher stood in front of me for several moments before saying to the entire class, "In all my years of teaching, nobody has ever gotten a perfect score on one of my exams." She stared at me with burning intensity, half-jokingly, yet with a very sharp edge to her voice asking, "Did you cheat?" as she set my graded test before me, marked 100%. I told her I'd been so sick that the only thing I did that day was take her test—I'd really been out of it. Her eyes flashed as she sized up my response, and I began to feel a sense of wonderment that I'd done so well on a test when I'd felt so very ill.

From St. Louis Housewife to Literary Star

One of the most prolific and popular writing prodigies of 20th century America was a most unlikely candidate. Pearl Lenore Curran, a Saint Louis housewife who'd received limited education and dropped out of school at age 13, became famous writing works under her pen name, Patience Worth. But this was no typical nom de plume—this was an actual persona Pearl believed she received her stories and poems from. Patience Worth became such a national phenomenon that in 1917, prestigious *Braithwaite* anthology listed five of her poems amongst the nation's best poetry published that year, and the

New York Times hailed Worth's first novel as a "feat of literary composition." Patience Worth was so prolific a writer that in addition to seven books she wrote volumes of poetry, short stories, plays, and reams of sparkling conversation coming to a total of some four million words written in a quarter century. Professor of philosophy Stephen Braude commented,

> *"What is extraordinary about this case is the fluidity, versatility, virtuosity and literary quality of Patience's writings."*

In addition to writing verse in the style of 17th century Patience Worth, Pearl also wrote a book from the time of Jesus Christ that included descriptions of sights, smells and sounds that were not known in Pearl's time, *The Sorry Tale*. This book is still in print today, and still remarkably popular, thanks to the way it gives readers the unmistakeable impression of reading an eye-witness account of events that played out thousands of years ago in Biblical times. This book is not primarily focused on Jesus Christ, but rather is an intricately woven tale of three main characters and the effects their words and actions had on those around them.

What prompted Pearl Curran's leap from bored housewife to writing prodigy? Pearl's impetus to write began quite by accident one evening after a dinner party, when Pearl and a friend picked up an Ouija board used to contact discarnate spirits, and Pearl began receiving detailed, lively communications from Patience Worth. The Ouija board became unnecessary after a while, as words flowed through after Pearl felt slight pressure in her head when she sensed Patience Worth's presence. Crowds of people flocked to Pearl's home to watch her amazing feats of literary productivity in action.

Great controversy erupted during Pearl's lifetime over the source of her literary gifts, with psychoanalyst Wilfrid Lay insisting that Patience's writing was merely "the automatic activities" of Pearls' unconscious. Philosopher Charles Cory wrote a long article in a 1919 edition of *Psychological Review* in which he asserted his opinion that Patience's writings could be explained by multiple personality. Cory admitted being confounded by the fact that Pearl Curran remained herself while Patience dictated to her, since multiple personalities typically only adopt personalities sequentially, one at a time, concluding that while Pearl went about her daily activities her "other self" composed her prose. Psychologist Walter Franklin Prince spent several weeks meeting with Pearl, reading through the entire Patience Worth record, and interviewing her friends and family. What's remarkable about Prince's visit is that at the time, he was known and feared as he worked with Harry Houdini to expose fake mediums—and he had been an amateur magician, as well as Episcopal and Methodist minister. Prince also had adopted a girl diagnosed with multiple personalities, yet he found Pearl Curran remarkable yet ordinary, concluding that Pearl had produced the Patience Worth material and that *"some cause operating through but not originating in... Mrs. Curran must be acknowledged."*

Pearl herself writes in *The Unpartizan Review*,

> *"Whatever may be the association which I describe as the presence of Patience Worth, it is one of the most beautiful that it can be the privilege of a human being to experience. Through this contact I have been educated to a deeper spiritual understanding and appreciation than I might have acquired in any study I can conceive of. Six years ago I could not have understood the literature of Patience Worth, had it been shown to me. And I doubt if it would have attracted me sufficiently to give me the desire to study it. The pictorial visions which accompany the coming of the words have acted as a sort of primer, and gradually developed within me a height of appreciation by*

persistently tempting my curiosity with representations of incidents and symbols. I am like a child with a magic picture book. Once I look upon it, all I have to do is to watch its pages open before me, and revel in their beauty and variety and novelty." Pearl continues, *"The picture is not confined to the point narrated, but takes in everything else within the circle of vision at the time. For instance, if two people are seen talking on the street, I see not only them, but the neighboring part of the street, with the buildings, stones, dogs, people and all, just as they would be in a real scene. (Or are these scenes actual reproductions?) If the people talk a foreign language, as in The Sorry Tale, I hear the talk, but over and above is the voice of Patience, either interpreting or giving me the part she wishes to use as story."*

One requirement for quantum jumping is that a kind of bridge from one time and place to another be established. Clearly, Pearl felt motivated to make a connection to someone from another reality... from another place in time. Even though we haven't yet been able to verify the identity of Patience Worth, we can sense her humanity, passion, and inspiration through her words. The fact that this information was transmitted across hundreds of years of time and thousands of miles through space provides us with a clear sense that Curran made a quantum jump that bridged completely separate worlds, and gifted her with world-class writing skills.

Pearl truly desired to make a connection with another reality, and found a way to relax with an open mind to experience alternate realities via the meditative and energizing use of an Ouija board. The Ouija board activated a detached state of mind that allowed Pearl to make a huge leap into an alternate space and time. Pearl had such a strong desire to experience a radically different reality than the one she'd been living prior to connecting with Patience Worth, and her ability to hold a clear vision of Patience Worth made this connection as long-lasting and remarkable as it was. And perhaps best of all, making a quantum jump to write with Patience Worth brought passion, purpose and joy into Pearl Curran's life. As Pearl writes in *The Unpartizan Review*,

> *"My own writing fatigues me, while the other (Patience Worth's) exhilarates me. That's a queer mess of a statement, but quite true."*

From Broken to Unbroken Leg

My friend, Susan, took a moonlit walk by herself one night while on a camping trip to Joshua Tree National Park with some friends. Relishing the excitement of jumping from rock to rock as she used to do as a young girl, Susan didn't notice she'd misjudged one jump, until she landed painfully on her right leg. She felt like her leg was broken, and when she visited the emergency room at the hospital, this news was confirmed by Susan's doctor who told her, *"You broke your fibula."* Because this hospital was a teaching hospital, a supervising doctor also examined Susan's X-rays, and confirmed the first doctor's assessment, saying to Susan, *"You've broken your fibular head."*

At this point, Susan called me and we spoke on the phone about her injury, and we did some energy work on her broken leg, to speed healing. I envisioned her leg being healthy with bones strong and unbroken, and at some point during our conversation, Susan told me she felt something like an itchiness where her fibula was broken. I told Susan, *"That's a very good sign! Feeling itchiness is often an indication of that part of the body healing."*

Later in the week, Susan went to her appointment for a follow-up visit at the clinic. While Susan was waiting, she asked a medic if she could please look at her X-rays while she waited.

He flipped on the viewing lights, granted her permission to see her X-rays, and left the room. Susan pulled two different X-rays out of the envelope and examined them closely. She couldn't see anything that looked like a break, crack or any other kind of disturbance, but figured to herself, *"I'm no doctor, and I'm not trained in reading X-rays. I probably just don't know what I'm looking for."*

When the orthopedic doctor entered the room, she said she'd just looked at my X-rays and didn't understand my diagnosis, since she didn't see a broken bone! She said she even asked the radiologist to look at them, and he didn't see anything, either. Susan found it amusing to watch her try to explain how this could happen. At first, it seemed like she was blaming the younger attending physician who'd first told Susan she broke her fibula when she was in the emergency room that Monday. But then, when Susan told her that not only did he look at her X-rays, but also the supervising physician confirmed Susan's leg was broken.

At this point, the doctor became flustered, not wanting to admit hospital error, while clearly confused about what had happened. She fiddled with Susan's leg—poking, twisting, prodding. While Susan flinched a bit, it was more because she was anticipating pain than actually feeling pain. When the doctor asked Susan if anything hurt, Susan told the doctor, *"It really only feels like someone is pressing on a bruise you might have received in some random way."* The doctor responded, *"Well, that's probably what you did. You might have just bruised the bone."* Not only was Susan's leg healed, but so were her original X-rays!

After Susan heard this rather startling announcement, she came home to search for her paperwork that had originally been sent home with her after her initial visit to the hospital. This paperwork was the standard care printout for "a broken extremity," and Susan recalled that further down there was mention of "a broken fibular head."

Susan told me while searching for the missing documentation, *"I need this paperwork to show my employers why I've been missing work and needed to visit the emergency room."* Susan's house was hardly a mess of paperwork, and she was quite annoyed to have lost the papers that could prove she hadn't made up the whole thing and taken so many days off work for no reason. A while later, while doing some house cleaning, Susan was surprised to find her missing paperwork... under her television set! She doesn't put anything there—it seemed like it had just suddenly appeared there!

From Dying of Cancer to Healthy Best-Selling Author

Some of the most inspirational quantum jumps have to do with miraculous healing, and come from people who've had near death experiences (NDEs). Author Anita Moorjani writes in her book, *Dying to Be Me*, about feeling she has reached a point of poor health by which family, friends and doctors considered her to be dying—yet after Anita had a near death experience, she emerged with newfound wonder and fearlessness. Anita credits her complete recovery and remission from cancer to having accessed a state of loving, lucid consciousness from which she could view all possible events of her past, present and future... knowing that when she has no fear, she had access to great power.

> *"While I was in that state of clarity in the other realm, I instinctively understood that I was dying because of all my fears. I wasn't expressing my true self because my worries were preventing me from doing so. I understood that the cancer wasn't a punishment or anything like that. It was just my own energy, manifesting as cancer because my*

fears weren't allowing me to express myself as the magnificent force I was meant to be."

People who witness spontaneous remissions such as Anita Moorjani's realize that such miracles can—and often do—happen in an instant. In her excellent book *Creating Miracles*, Carolyn Miller describes how people have faced potentially lethal situations and avoided victimization by realizing in the midst of their ordeal that they could find and project a higher state of awareness on the situation. Their feelings changed their situations so much that would-be muggers and rapists walked away from potential victims, and a car plummeting off the side of the road landed safely in a lake... that had never been there before.

Miller tells numerous true stories that all share a common thread... in a time of need, people can and do create miracles. All that is needed is an attitude of love and "miracle mindedness." This attitude can overcome even the most horrific situations, bringing compassion to individuals who otherwise would show no mercy, and shifting reality in very profound ways.

Miller reviews dozens of stories to find some common threads... some ways that people have found to shift reality in these times of great stress: Feel love and move beyond the limited perspective of ego's worries and fears, expect a positive or neutral outcome, and feel a meditative sense of detached, non-judgmental peacefulness. By practicing achieving a meditative state on a regular basis, being optimistic, and being loving, we can predispose ourselves to experiencing wonderful miracles. When we mindfully enter a pure energy state, we can choose which reality we select next.

Those of us who've experienced shifts in reality involving keys, wallets, socks, and other objects disappearing from one

134

location and appearing in another have witnessed quantum jumps of macroscopic objects moving through space—or teleporting—outside of scientific laboratories. These real life experiences can be observed the way biologists observe animal behavior in the wild, since such events occur naturally, rather than as predictable outcomes from laboratory studies. We can write journal entries about what we witnessed as reality shifted, in similar fashion to the kind of field notes a scientist watching wild animals would keep. We can pay attention to what emotional states we're feeling during times when reality shifts, and what kinds of emotions are most conducive to more enjoyable shifts in reality.

How to Realize... or Not Realize... Fears

Pamela wrote to me about one of her most memorable experiences while living in the Mojave Desert. She and her husband were both stationed at the Naval Hospital in Twentynine Palms, California at the time, when they drove one Thanksgiving weekend to a Borders bookstore that was about a 90 minute drive from home. Pamela and her husband had recently had a string of bad luck with vehicles breaking down, and Pamela became increasingly apprehensive that their one operational vehicle, her husband's old Toyota Trooper, would break down and leave them stranded.

Pamela couldn't shake off this fear, until she voiced to her husband how much she'd hate it if the truck broke down. Though they arrived at Borders without incident, the truck started making unusual noises after only half an hour on the return trip home.

When they pulled off the freeway and into a gas station, the Trooper died completely. No auto shops were open on that Thanksgiving weekend, so Pamela and her husband walked to an ATM to get some money for a motel for the night... but neither of their ATM cards worked in any of three separate ATMs they walked to... though their cards had worked earlier that same day.

With only $5 in cash and no way to pay for a hotel, they walked back to sleep in the truck. It was cold and miserable, and Pamela marveled how she'd been rendered powerless by a few small circumstances—a broken-down truck and non-operational ATM cards. As time seemed to slow down, Pamela felt like she'd created the whole situation. Instead of getting angry or depressed like she usually would when not in 'control,' she felt an amazing sense of peace and well-being. Pamela decided to just allow things to happen, while being present and calm enough to observe and participate in their unfolding. This was a new way of being Pamela hadn't experienced before.

Pamela was sitting in the driver's seat when dawn finally came. She glanced over at her husband to see if he was still asleep, and saw him open his eyes as he said, "Turn the key." Pamela had a moment of doubt and was just about to open her mouth and remind him they'd already turned the key a hundred times, when she saw something in his eyes that stopped her. She turned the key, and the truck started! They were grateful to be able to drive home with no problems. Their truck ran just fine, and their ATM cards worked, too.

Pamela wrote to me that she came to a deeper realization about a lot of things after this experience. Pamela no longer allows herself to fear anything, because she now knows she can easily create the very thing she fears, finding herself face-to-face with it. This experience helped Pamela realize,

"If I can create the things I fear, I must be able to create the things I desire as well."

Car Crash Avoided

George wrote to me from East Jordan, Michigan, to tell me how he took too sharp a turn around a blind corner one winter, and ended up in the same lane as an oncoming vehicle. George's brakes locked up as his car and and the other bore down on a collision course toward one another. Just at the point that a crash seemed inevitable, when the cars were only one feet apart, suddenly George's car was six feet back, allowing just enough time to avert disaster. George commented, *"It was as if I had traded places with another quantum version of myself... one who had left the house seconds after I had."*

Surviving Steel Beams Falling All Around

Scott, was about 21 years old and working as a trucker when he had a truly life-changing experience. He'd driven a semi load of scrap iron from Lewiston, Idaho to Clarkston, Washington. Since Scott was responsible for 'settling the load' he'd delivered once it arrived, Scott was standing atop the receiving trailer, where he eased each 5-ton steel beam down in a stable position in a pile as the crane operator lowered each beam down, one by one.

After about half the truckload of steel beams were piled and with another slowly descending, the chain holding the beam glitched and came loose. The beam free fell some twenty feet where it struck beams at the top of the load, landing crossways and just missing Scott's head by a foot. The crashing beam jarred the piled beams loose, so the whole lot tumbled to the ground off the semi trailer, with Scott in the middle of it all.

When Scott told his mom about this incident the next day, Brenda asked, *"What did you do?"* and he said, *"I went into 'auto-pilot,' Mom. There was nothing I could do, so I hugged my*

arms as tight as I could and I said, 'Oh God, thank you for my life!
Oh God, thank you for my life!' over and over and over again."

Once all the beams had stopped crashing down, the crane operator carefully lifted the pile of steel beams one by one off of Scott. The crane operator could not believe his eyes—there wasn't one single scratch on Scott anywhere, not even a bump on the head. Scott did have blood blisters that remained for five days on the back of both his arms, where he'd hugged himself so tightly during the beam loading accident.

Teleported to Safety

Amy wrote to me about a remarkable incident that occurred one day when she was living in Philadelphia and working at a home improvement supply store. Amy took the bus each day to and from work, with a bus stop conveniently located just a few blocks from her house. One morning, Amy walked up to where she crossed to reach the bus stop at the corner of the main road in Roxborough, and heard the sound of screeching tires coming her way. Despite this sound being off in the distance, Amy felt it might be unsafe to cross. She was standing at the corner at that time, when she saw the vehicle approaching the intersection, poised to make a left turn. Amy knew the car would jump the curb where she stood, so she shut her eyes.

When she felt no impact, Amy opened her eyes to find she was now several feet before the curb behind a small tree. From this safe vantage point, she saw the car approach the intersection again, and attempt the left turn all over again! But this time, Amy saw the car hit the curb exactly where she'd been standing several seconds ago before skidding up the sidewalk to stop at the tree she was standing behind. Amy wrote, *"I had a feeling like I was just floating, and I was stunned—shocked to the core!"*

Car Traveled Through Two-Lane Concrete Abutment

My friend Clipper told me about an extraordinary experience that happened to him while driving a 1947 Super Clipper in November 1972. He had been driving for many hours, traveling east on Highway 40 through Wyoming toward Chicago, having just come through part of Colorado, when it began to lightly snow. Realizing he'd become quite drowsy, Clipper knew it was time to stop, so he pulled the car all the way across the road to the left, so the car's headlights would be pointing toward oncoming traffic traveling in the opposite direction, and wouldn't provide drunk drivers with something they might try to follow (and collide with).

Almost immediately after Clipper had pulled over to the side of the road, he fell asleep. A couple of hours later, he woke up and got out of the car to stretch. Looking around, he noticed his car's set of tire tracks in the snow and walked alongside them toward the overpass abutment behind the car. They led directly to the concrete overpass abutment. Clipper thought, *"This is impossible, there has to be a gap with no tire tracks, and space for the bumper,"* and, *"If the car came through the overpass, is there a door here somewhere?"*

He walked under the overpass, some 40 feet to the other side of the concrete abutment, where he saw a set of tire tracks coming off the highway and leading directly up to the abutment. The tire tracks in the snow were clear, with only a light dusting of snow having fallen since they'd been made. Astonishingly, the tracks clearly led from Highway 40 up to the concrete and steel two-lane overpass abutment... where they picked up again directly on the other side, leading all the way to the car. There were no other marks or footprints to indicate someone had moved the car or played an elaborate prank of creating tire tracks leading all the way up to and from the abutment, as if it hadn't been there at all.

Bilocating Quantum Jumping

On September 30, 2007, I was working indoors at a full-day holistic expo in Concord, California, gazing out one of the windows on that sunny day, daydreaming I was actually out enjoying a walk on a street in a favorite neighborhood on that beautiful day. A short while later, I received an email from my friend Katrina, who told me that she had seen me walking down Solano Avenue in Albany that day. She was excited to tell me about this because she knew I was scheduled to be attending a full-day holistic expo out of town that day, and she was therefore quite surprised to have seen me strolling down the street so many miles away.

Many years earlier, I'd woken up one cold morning and decided to stay in bed and enjoy the warmth and quiet of the household a bit, before getting up and awakening my two young daughters. In that delicious hypnagogic state between waking and dreaming, I imagined I was doing my usual daily routine of getting out of bed, walking down the hall, opening the door to my daughters' room, walking over to their window and opening the window shade, and greeting them with a pleasant, *"Good morning! Time to rise and shine!"* Several minutes passed as I continued resting under the warm covers, and then I was surprised to hear some noise down the hall... then the pitter-patter of two pairs of little feet... then the voices of my very surprised daughters, asking me what I was doing back in bed. *"Back in bed?"* I asked, with just as much confusion as they were showing me. They told me I'd come into their room and woken them up. When I asked, *"Did I open your window shade?"* they replied *"Yes!"* and I got up to see for myself that their window shade was indeed now fully open—something neither of them was tall enough to accomplish themselves.

Our parallel selves can really get things done sometimes, and it can feel like you've just cloned yourself and are now operating at maximum efficiency! I was recognized for an ability similar to what Nicolas Cage's character, Cris Johnson, does in the 2007 movie, *Next*, when I worked at Citibank as a project manager back in the 1980s. Just as Nicolas Cage's character, Cris, is able to mentally walk through a maze of future possibilities, following each probable future thread through to either its abrupt conclusion or path forward to the next auspicious decision point, so too could I consistently choose to most efficiently only take action on projects that weren't dead ends. I focused exclusively on the projects, people, and tasks that were worth devoting my time, effort, and energy to. Needless to say, this skill, though invisible to others, was definitely noticed by management, who often mentioned in my employee reviews that I did the work of many people. From my perspective, I was simply choosing the brightest options.

Whether we call these experiences bilocation, teleportation, or lucid living, they provide us with wonderful examples of quantum jumping between different realities.

Teleportation Quantum Jumping

Throughout the course of history there have been several documented cases of quantum jumping in the form of teleportation. One of the most remarkable accounts began more than four hundred years ago in southeast Asia.

On October 24, 1593, Gil Pérez was on duty working as a palace guard in Manilla in the Philippines the day after he'd received word that Chinese pirates had killed Governor Gomez Perez Dasmarinas. Gil Pérez closed his eyes and leaned against a wall to rest, and when he opened his eyes he found himself in Mexico City's Plaza Mayor, over 9,000 miles away, wearing the uniform of the guards of the Del Gobernador Palace and with absolutely no idea how he came to be there. When questioned,

Pérez explained he had just been in Manilla earlier that same day, and he shared the news of the Governor's death, which was confirmed in Mexico a couple of months later when a ship arrived from the Philippines.

Another documented case of teleportation occurred in Europe in the year 1904. Signor Mauro Pansini, an Italian building contractor, witnessed his two sons vanishing from their home and being reported as having suddenly appeared many miles away on numerous occasions. Father Vannetti at the Capuchin Convent, at Malfatti, thirty miles away telephoned Signor Pansini one morning to inform him that ten year old Afredo and eight year old Paulo were there, and needed to be brought home. Pansini wondered how his sons could have traveled over thirty miles in less than half an hour as he arrived at the Convent to find his boys waiting in the reception hall. According to monks at the Convent, the boys arrived mysteriously, in a trance something like a deep hypnotic state. Signor Pansini took his sons home to their room, where he asked them to remain for the rest of the day. A few minutes after seeing them to bed, he decided to check on them and was astonished to find they had vanished out of a closed room! At that same moment, 15 miles away, Signor Pansini's brother heard a knock on his door, and found his dazed nephews wondering where they were.

Time Travel Quantum Jumping

Brad Steiger shares the experience recounted by Charles W. Ingersoll of Cloquet, Minnesota, who once was filmed leaning over the rim of the Grand Canyon, taking photographs with his 35mm camera. This film sequence appears in a 1948 Castle Films travelogue. Ingersoll actually made his first-ever trip to the Grand Canyon in 1955, when he brought his brand new camera that he'd purchased that very year. When Ingersoll returned from his Grand Canyon vacation, he was astonished to find, purchase and watch this travelogue dating seven years earlier that clearly showed him at the Grand Canyon in 1948— holding a camera that wouldn't be created until 1955.

*   *   *

The next chapter, *Get a Quantum Jump Start*, shares tips from recent scientific studies and reports of quantum jumps that have changed peoples' lives for the better when they made simple changes to their behavior. These are the kinds of behavioral changes you might wish to make to be more like your imagined best possible future self—happy, healthy, confident, and enjoying life to the fullest. If you've ever wondered how and when it helps to "fake it 'til you make it," you'll definitely want to read every page of Chapter Five!

Exercise

Breathing Intentions Meditation

Start this meditation by setting the intention that what you wish to attract, you'll attract. You can set intentions as simply as breathing, being mindful and honest with yourself about what you need and how you feel.

(1) As you breathe in, imagine you are inhaling what you need in your life, thinking, *"I'm getting what I need."*

(2) As you breathe out, imagine you are exhaling how you feel... letting those emotions and energies flow through and out of you, thinking, *"I'm giving how I feel."*

(3) Keep breathing with each inhalation expressing your conscious intent to receive what you need, and each exhalation representing how you feel.

(4) Once you've breathed deeply and fully several times, you start to gain better understanding of how and what you're creating in your life. Conscious creation is a process of shifting your intentions through resetting what you need and how you feel—you can have conscious input into both of these things.

(5) With conscious intent, imagine you are breathing in more enjoyable levels of what you need in your life, as you think, *"I'm getting what I need."*

(6) With conscious intent, imagine you are breathing out a more enjoyable level of how you feel in your life, thinking, *"I'm giving how I feel."*

(7) As you set your intention for what you need and consciously breathe these energies into yourself, this simple meditation allows you to become more mindful and balanced.

Exercise

Describe a Reality Shift Experience

Remember a time when something appeared, disappeared, transformed or transported... or you observed a change in the experience of time. Think of an experience in which someone you trust recalled something completely different than how you know events occurred, yet they insisted their version of events was accurate. Consider a time when an amazing coincidence or synchronicity occurred, or someone or something was healed remarkably fast. Write down all the details you can recall from your reality shift experiences, including date, time, place, and people involved. If other people were involved who also experienced a reality shift with you, contact them and ask them to share with you what they remember of the sequence of events—and request that they share this with you without first reading or reviewing your recollection of what transpired.

*"It is never too late to be
what you might have been."*
—George Eliot

Chapter 5

Get a Quantum

Jump Start

If you're wondering whether quantum jumping is something you can do, this chapter is designed to reassure you that you're already quantum jumping most every day. Quantum jumping, like any skill, can be improved by paying attention to when and how it works, and what you can do to best utilize the idea of making leaps into new realities.

Anyone who's ever "faked it 'til they make it" has given quantum jumping a shot, simply by adopting the speech, mannerism, dress, and other aspects of the person they wish to become. Quantum jumping is not an exercise in inauthenticity, but rather a skill that helps you make the leap from current to desired realities. Your expectations, beliefs and perspective can build up your confidence in a number of practical ways. Learning to take positive actions and behave like the version of you who is relaxed, smart, and confident can confer these qualities to you.

Many examples of simple things you can do that provide you with a running start and flying leap into the realities you'd most enjoy are provided in this chapter. Often, the most important step to make toward attaining a goal is the first one, with all others being much easier once forward motion is begun. As Lao Tzu once said, *"A journey of a thousand miles begins with a single step."*

It's easier to believe techniques are practical and really function when they've been tested and proven, so the quantum jumping tips included in this chapter are backed up by scientific studies confirming that they work. By taking a few simple actions like the ones suggested in this chapter, you can be well on your way on your own personal journey to reducing feelings of stress, increasing confidence, and even falling in and staying in love.

The Science of Faking It 'Til You Make It

If such a thing as the science of "faking it 'til you make it" exists—and indeed it does—we'd expect to find it in the fields of sociology and psychology. American sociologist Robert King Merton coined the expression "self-fulfilling prophecy," which he explained as being:

"a prediction about the outcome of a situation can invoke new behavior that leads to the prediction coming true."

Put another way, it's as if we walk into another world of possibility the moment we make the decision to think, talk, and behave differently. So how can this help to make us make the jump to being more healthy, wealthy, happy and wise? Finding some scientific studies to support that any of these things are attainable through quantum jumping would be marvelous— and as it turns out, a growing body of such scientific evidence exists.

Why Be Happy?

Numerous studies have shown that happy people are successful across many areas of their lives—including in marriage, friendship, income, work performance, and health. UC Riverside psychology professor Sonja Lyubomirsky proposes that the happiness-success link runs two directions, so not only does success make people happy, but positive affect promotes success. Lyubomirsky and her colleagues found that happiness doesn't just feel good—it is at the heart of most everything we treasure most, and really does translate to greater overall prosperity in life.

Benefits of happiness include: higher income and superior work outcomes with greater productivity and higher quality of work; larger social rewards thanks to longer-lasting, happier marriages, more friends, and richer social interactions; more activity, energy and flow, and better physical health with a stronger immune system, lower stress, and less pain; and even longer life. Happy people are more creative, helpful, charitable, and self-confident. They have better self-control, and show better self-regulatory and coping abilities.

The field of positive psychology is showing us how happiness improves so many qualities of life as it helps us see the world more expansively, with reduced stress, depression, anxiety and fear. When we're happy, we attract positive people to us who love being near us and helping us.

Enjoy Pleasant Distractions When Life Gets You Down

Humans may or may not be the only species that can reflect upon themselves, but such self-reflection when feeling sad can be a negative thing. As it turns out, ruminating on what went wrong and reviewing the whole sorry history of "mistakes" from our past can do a lot more harm than good. Recent studies indicate we're far better off doing something that engages us in pleasant or neutral distraction than dwell on negative thoughts. Such distractions activate our ability to feel inspired in fresh new ways so we can solve problems, as we become absorbed with engaging activities. So instead of replaying some slow-motion remembered train wreck in the theater of your mind one more time, get up and do something that stops that brooding cycle.

The key to making proper use of distractions is to do something different when you notice you're feeling upset. Going for a walk, getting some exercise, playing a game, or visiting with friends can help you gain a fresh point of view with regard to any adversity you've recently encountered. Not only can proper use of an entertaining distraction help prevent you from slipping into depression, but it can also help you move little by little to a higher state of optimism, which is associated with better health and longevity.

To ensure you try out some pleasant distractions, think of a type of situation you encounter anywhere from once in a while to fairly often that could benefit from a helpful distraction now and again. Rehearse how you can utilize a distraction successfully in the future, the next time a similar situation arises. Get a clear picture of yourself taking a break from whatever you're doing the next time you feel sad. Envision what kind of positive distraction you can enjoy, and picture yourself doing that. This simple process of envisioning specific trigger situations and actual things you can do will help you enjoy a pleasant distraction next time it can be beneficial to you.

Write Down What Went Well Today

One of the best things you can do is to make regular daily time for meditation or prayer, focusing primarily on feeling acceptance and gratitude. Such a positive focus when reinforced on a regular, daily basis can release you from identifying with painful or traumatic events recalled from the past.

Take ten minutes at the end of each day to write down a few wonderful moments from your day, along with why they went well that you had something to do with. Make sure to give yourself credit for having some of the qualities you most appreciate in yourself, such as: Gratitude, Love, Kindness, Honesty, Bravery, Creativity, Hope, Zest, and Perseverance.

This what-went-well exercise has been proven in a series of controlled psychological research studies to make a huge positive difference in peoples' lives. Dr. Martin Seligman, the "Father of Positive Psychology," reports that fifty of the most severely depressed people who participated in one of his studies experienced a remarkable reduction in depression after just one week of doing the what-went-well exercise. Seligman reports,

"On average, their depression score plummeted from 34 to 17, from extreme to the cusp of mild-moderate, and their happiness score jumped from the 15th percentile to the 50th percentile. Forty-seven of the fifty were now less depressed and happier."

If you or someone close to you is depressed, this simple practice of writing down what-went-well each day can make a tremendous difference. Considering the potential benefits from writing down what-went-well, it is well worth making a few minutes for this exercise at the end of every day.

Smile and Feel Happier

Many recent scientific studies confirm that faking it 'til we make it works for increasing happiness. Smile studies show that people consistently feel happier when simulating smiles—

pretending to smile—regardless how happy they actually felt. One of the earliest such studies by German psychologist Fritz Strack showed how simply putting a pen between one's teeth (thereby artfully moving facial muscles into a fairly good approximation of a smile position) caused study participants to laugh more while viewing cartoons than study participants who'd put the pen between their lips (simulating forced frowns). Strack's study participants were told a deceptive cover story about the purpose of the research being for studying adaptations for people who'd lost use of their hands. Aside from this slight change in initial experimental explanations, study participants were otherwise treated the same... yet those who placed the pen between their teeth laughed more when looking at the cartoons. Scientists believe the reason people actually do end up feeling happier after faking a smile is that even small changes in facial expression can be powerful enough to create discernible transformations in the autonomic nervous system.

The innovative Strack study was redone in 2002 with the same slightly deceptive cover story (helping people who'd lost use of their hands) by Robert Soussignan, this time with study participants holding pens in their mouth and teeth in one of four different ways: in the lips with no smile, in the teeth with no smile, in the teeth with fake smile, and in the teeth with stretched corners of the mouth and raised cheeks (full fake smile). Soussingnan's findings supported Strack's earlier study, confirming that study participants who smiled more fully laughed and enjoyed watching cartoons much more later on. Smile research is excellent news for those with treatment-resistant depression, providing new hope for people suffering from depression.

Intriguingly, some studies show that Botox treatments fight depression—but only when applied to certain areas of a person's face. Botox treatments appear to have the power to either relieve or exacerbate depression in those who undergo the cosmetic surgery, depending on exactly where the Botox injections are applied. Symptoms of depression are reduced when Botox treatments continue to permit Botox treatment recipients to easily smile, and when removing "frown lines" on recipients' foreheads. If the Botox injections interfere in part of the musculature involved in smiling, such as removal of crow's feet (also known as 'smile lines') around the eyes, patients report feeling increasingly depressed after their Botox treatments. Removal of frown lines by Botox treatment has been found to relieve depression, provided recipients were still able to smile.

Dr. Michael Lewis of the School of Psychology in Cardiff, Wales reported that people with crows' feet Botox treatment experienced much more depression than those who merely received Botox injection treatments for frown lines. Noting that Botox can influence patients' ability to make particular expressions, Dr. Lewis said, *"The expressions that we make on our face affects the emotions we feel; we smile because we are happy, but smiling also makes us happy. Treatment with drugs like Botox prevents the patient from being able to make a particular expression."* Further research investigating just why the expressions we are able to make on our face have such a pronounced impact on mood is needed. Swiss psychiatrist M. Axel Wollmer believes use of the Botox treatment *"interrupts feedback from the facial musculature to the brain, which may be involved in the development and maintenance of negative emotions."*

The big practical idea from all this smile research is that smiling lifts your spirits, even if you're forcing your smiles (with a pen in your mouth), or have had Botox treatments that prevent you from frowning.

Become More Outgoing for a Happier Life

Studies show that extroverts are generally happier than introverts, so a scientifically proven method to feel happier through changing behavior is simply to *act* more like an extrovert. Social psychologist William Fleeson reports that people who tracked their moods over the course of two weeks reported feeling happier when they acted outgoing and reported feeling less happy when their behavior was quiet and reserved. Fleeson and his colleagues found that,

> *"Every single participant in the study was happier when he or she acted extroverted than when he or she acted introverted."*

It may seem surprising that happiness—something we feel on the inside—can be so strongly influenced by how we interact with others on the outside... yet this appears to be the case. Fleeson explains,

> *"As a society, we tend to think of happiness as something that comes from outside us. It's kind of a radical idea that we have some control of happiness, that personality is a factor in happiness, and that, to some extent, we have control over our personalities."*

Dr. Catharine Gale of the University of Southampton worked with teams from the University of Edinburgh and University College London to investigate long-term influence of personality traits in youth on happiness and satisfaction later in life. Dr. Gale and her team studied nearly 4,600 people over the span of more than five decades, and their findings are remarkable. Dr. Gale reports that, *"Extroversion in youth had direct, positive effects on well-being and life satisfaction in later life."* With regard to the significance of these findings, Dr. Gale explains,

"Understanding what determines how happy people feel in later life is of particular interest because there is good evidence that happier people tend to live longer."

Now that the 'big five traits' in psychology (openness-to-experience, conscientiousness, extroversion, agreeableness, and neuroticism) are being recognized as much more malleable than previously thought, psychologists are more aware than ever that people are not permanently one way or the other, but instead can develop introvert or extrovert qualities. Introverts love reading books, taking walks, and doing things on their own, whereas extroverts adore parties and opportunities to get feedback from others. People have been observed to make many changes to the 'big five traits' over the course of their lives.

Extroverts are noted for being more highly motivated than introverts, which probably naturally stems from their heightened awareness of feedback from others. In two separate studies in which 150 college students were randomly assigned to behave as introverts or extroverts. Of those students who were asked to behave counter to their natural inclinations, extroverts performed worse on cognitive tests when acting like introverts, whereas introverts acting like extroverts showed no such diminishment... either cognitively, or in terms of negative emotional effects.

"We didn't find a lot of evidence for... the idea that acting like an extrovert would wear out introverts," said Dr. John Zelenski, a psychologist at Carleton University in Ottowa. *"We found acting like an introvert tended to wear out extroverts."*

Based on studies to date, it seems pretty clear that if you're already an extrovert, you're doing just fine—stay just as extroverted as you are. If you are naturally introverted, these same studies would indicate you might feel happier simply by behaving more like an extrovert. It's certainly easy enough to give it a try! Accept social invitations, talk to more strangers, and spend more time with other people. Make an effort to meet and greet people you don't know, and ask them how they're doing. Keep a journal so you can see for yourself what a difference becoming more sociable makes for you.

Strike a Power Pose for Greater Confidence

Not only can you boost happiness through faking it 'til you make it—you can boost your personal feeling of and social perceptions of power through your body posture. And the best news is that when you start to act powerfully, you start to think powerfully, even some time after striking an expansive, empowering pose. Benefits go far beyond simply feeling better to include: performing better in interviews, coping more effectively with stressful situations, and making better impressions.

Harvard social psychologist Amy J.C. Cuddy didn't originally intend to be one of the world's top researchers in the field of social psychology. Her fascination with the way the mind and body interact arose from being hospitalized with severe head trauma after riding in a car whose driver fell asleep doing 90 miles per hour. Cuddy's brain injury left her having to relearn how to learn, taking years off from school while wondering if her IQ would ever be the same. Fortunately, Cuddy's IQ was restored after two years, so she was able to return to dancing and school.

Cuddy conducted a study with 42 male and female participants who were randomly assigned to either high-power or low-power pose groups... with study participants being intentionally misinformed that the study had to do with placement of ECG electrodes near their hearts. High-power group participants were manipulated to adopt one of two expansive poses for one minute each, including the classic feet-on-desk-with-hands-behind-head, and standing and leaning on one's hands over a desk. The low-power participants were directed to pose in two restrictive poses: sitting in a chair with arms close and hands folded, and standing with arms and legs crossed tightly. Measurements of subjects' pre and post-study cortisol and testosterone levels showed that high-power poses decreased cortisol by about 25% and increased testosterone by 19% in both men and women. In sharp contrast, low-power poses increased cortisol about 17% and decreased testosterone by 10%. Both male and female high-power posers reported feeling more powerful and in charge, with those in the high-power group more likely to risk taking a chance with a $2 gamble with 86% of high-power participants rolling the die, compared to just 60% of the low-power posers.

In a more recent study, Cuddy and her colleagues at Harvard Business School conducted an experiment to determine whether adopting and holding expansive power poses for a period of seven minutes prior to being interviewed produced subsequent gains in speech quality (intelligent, clear, well-constructed content) or presentation quality (enthusiastic, confident, and captivating). Cuddy and her colleagues found that participants who engaged in preparatory power posing got higher interview scores and were more enthusiastic, confident, and captivating... yet they were not found to make more intelligent, clear or well-constructed presentations. Amazingly, those who practiced the power poses prior to being interviewed had similar body postures to those that didn't have such power posing preparation—yet they felt more empowered and were more often chosen to be hired by the interviewers. As Cuddy and her colleagues summarize their findings,

> "This suggests that preparatory power posing can serve as a simple, free, nonverbal tool that has the potential to be adopted by and beneficial to almost anyone, including those who are chronically powerless due to lack of physical resources or hierarchical status."

As you might suspect, it is possible to over-do the power posing. Some power moves can be interpreted by others as lacking warmth and trustworthiness, especially with types of movements that come across as overly assertive. Amy Cuddy cautions against using such alpha "cowboy" moves as sitting with legs apart and one arm draped on a nearby chair. Trustworthiness and warmth are conveyed through body language by natural smiles and friendly touches to peoples' shoulders or arms. Since the benefits of power posing have a carry-over effect, they can be done in private settings before getting together with others in social settings, for beneficial effects without causing inadvertent social problems.

With modern day technological devices getting tinier and tinier, what effect does our having the latest gadget have on how we behave and are perceived? Cuddy and her colleague Maarten Bos conducted a small scale study at the Harvard Decision

Sciences Lab to find out. 75 study participants were randomly assigned to interact with one of four electronic devices of varying size: an iPod Touch, an iPad, a MacBook Pro (laptop computer), or an iMac (desktop computer). As Cuddy hypothesized, people who worked on the smaller devices (including iPods and iPads) behaved less assertively—waiting longer to interrupt an experimenter who had made them wait, or not interrupting at all.

The useful aspect of this research is that once we know that smaller devices tend to make us behave less assertively (often without our noticing we've changed), we can minimize their use before doing anything where our social interactions are being assessed. Cuddy and Bos close by writing,

> *"We suggest that some time before going into a meeting, and obviously also during it, you put your cell phone away."*

You can try out these power poses for fun some time when you're by yourself where you won't feel self-conscious. Remember that these poses can be extremely helpful any time you need extra courage to make a phone call, write an email, or deal with challenging situations or people. In addition to turning off and putting your smaller techno-gadgets away, give yourself a few minutes to strike and hold an assertive pose— even if you're all alone and nobody's watching—and see whether you feel just a little bit more confident.

Increase Confidence by Sitting Up Straight

Do you remember a time when you were a child that you were asked by your parents or grandparents to, *"Sit up straight!"* They may not have given much of a reason for why that's such a good thing to do, but some researchers, such as Ohio State

University psychology professor Richard Petty, are delighted to explain the amazing hidden power of good sitting posture.

Petty explains, *"Most of us were taught that sitting up straight gives a good impression to other people. But it turns out that our posture can also affect how we think about ourselves. If you sit up straight, you end up convincing yourself by the posture you're in."*

Under the guise of participating in two different experiments simultaneously—one organized by the business school, and another by the arts school—participants in Petty's study were instructed to maintain specific acting postures while performing various business activities. The specific postures included either sitting up straight with chest pushed out, or sitting slouched forward with their face looking at their knees. While holding either of these two poses, study participants listed either three positive or three negative personal traits pertaining to future professional performance on a prospective job, and then rated themselves in a survey on how well they thought they would do as a future professional employee.

Amazingly, the students holding upright, confident postures in this study rated themselves in line with whatever positive or negative traits they'd written down, while the students who adopted the slumped-over pose had less confidence in what they'd written. Petty emphasized that researchers at no point used the words "confident" or "doubt" when giving instructions to participants, nor did they give any indication of how various postures might make them feel.

Improve Your Life by Becoming What You Think

When you think of old people, what are the first five words or phrases that come to mind? It turns out that your answer to this question could make a tremendous difference in your health and longevity in later years.

160

Recent research shows that our subconsciously adopted "age stereotypes" regarding our expectations of what will happen as we age makes a tremendous difference in how we actually do age. An increasing body of scientific research studies show that when seniors expect that growing older means they will become incapacitated, confused, useless, weak or devalued they are less likely to take preventive steps against such deterioration and they actually will suffer from mental and physical deterioration.

Intriguingly, when seniors believe positive stereotypes about aging, such as that older adults are wise, involved with life and satisfied, such individuals actually experience higher levels of physical and mental wellbeing. A medical research team at Yale University led by Becca Levy reported recently in *The Journal of the American Medical Association* that seniors with positive biases toward aging are 44% more likely to fully recover from a bout of disability—better able to bathe, dress and walk than those with negative aging stereotypes. The research team propose that positive age stereotypes are so effective because they operate through several pathways: limiting cardiovascular responses to stress, improving physical balance, enhancing self-efficacy, and increasing peoples' engagement in healthy behaviors.

Dr. Becca Levy is a pioneer in the field of age stereotypes and aging, and has helped us better appreciate the importance of maintaining a positive mindset around our elders, because their exposure—even subliminally—to negative age stereotypes and expectations can prove debilitating. Levy conducted many laboratory experiments with older people to observe peoples' reactions to subliminal messages prior to attempting to complete various tasks. Levy noted that seniors who'd subliminally received negative words, such as "decrepit" had worse handwriting and slower walking speeds afterward, whereas those who saw positive words such as "wisdom" did much better.

Dr. Levy studied a database of 600 people who'd been tracked over a period of 23 years, from 1975 to 1998, to see how people's age stereotypes influence their lives. Levy noted that participants with positive age stereotypes lived an average of 7.5 years longer than those with negative stereotypes. This longevity gap persisted even after variables of age, gender, socioeconomic status, loneliness and functional health were considered as covariates. Participants were asked at the beginning of the research to answer either "True" or "False" to questions such as, "Things keep getting worse as I get older," or "as you get older, you get less useful."

Dr. Levy asks us to be more mindful of the 'little things' that add to quite a lot when we interact with seniors. Everything from our tone of voice, attitude, and use of loaded phrases or expressions make a huge difference. Rather than parroting whatever negative stereotypes we might have accumulated, each of us has an opportunity to *think about how to reinforce the more positive aspects of aging,"* as Dr. Levy suggests.

Ask yourself again, when you think of old people, what are the first five words or phrases that come to mind? Hopefully you're now adopting some new, positive stereotypes about the elderly! Pay attention to seniors who demonstrate these positive qualities, and imagine how you and your loved ones can get better and better with each passing year.

Reduce Pain by Seeing Your Healthiest Self

Dr. Candida "Candy" McCabe made a stunning discovery with her team of researchers at the Royal National Hospital for Rheumatic Diseases and School for Health at the University of Bath in the United Kingdom, when they introduced a drug-free treatment that works on people suffering from complex regional pain syndrome (CRPS) and repetitive strain injury (RSI). These people often suffer pain so severe that no drugs have any appreciable effect, frustrating physicians and caregivers, and leaving those afflicted feeling hopeless and depressed in addition to the steady pain they feel that never seems to go away. McCabe's drug-free treatment works by tricking the brain into correcting its distorted image of the body—and it reduces pain using mirrors.

Dr. McCabe began her work as a research nurse investigating cases of rheumatoid arthritis in which patients perceived joint swelling, but where medical staff could find no physical evidence of swelling. Dr. McCabe and her team found that a simple system of providing patients with mirror visual feedback relieves their phantom limb pain. This treatment consists of a patient sitting along the edge of a mirror in such a way that their healthy side is reflected in a composite image showing a body with both the left and right sides healthy and pain-free. This visual illusion provides patients with a kind of corrective sensory feedback that allows them to see themselves as healthy, whole, and pain-free. McCabe believes pain often results from a mismatch in the way the brain perceives the body and the actual condition of the body. This sort of mismatch can occur when people are fitted with casts. "When the arm is immovable in a plaster cast a mismatch occurs, the brain sends out signals to the arm, but gets nothing back, so it triggers its own pain sensation in response."

While a majority of people with pain inside the cast feel better the moment their casts come off, about one third of those feeling pain continue to feel it, long after the cast is gone. *The mirror tricks the brain into resetting its body image and stops the pain,*" McCabe says. McCabe and her team have helped cure many people successfully with the mirror therapy technique, with some people requiring a number of treatments before being completely relieved from pain.

If you have pain on one side of your body but not the other, mirror visual feedback might make a positive difference for you. One of the perks of this treatment is that relatively little special equipment is required, aside from a large mirror, and it's something that almost anyone can do at home.

Reduce Pain by Hugging Yourself

Neuroscientist Giandomenico Iannetti from London's University College conducted a study in 2011 in which a team of scientists inflicted pain in a sensitive area of the study participants' forearms with radiant heat from an infrared laser. The intriguing part of this study involved testing the research hypothesis that when people crossed their arms, they'd feel less pain. Indeed, this proved to be the case, and not only did the study participants with crossed arms feel less pain when toasted by a laser, but they also felt fewer effects from electrically-evoked non-painful sensations. The researchers concluded that *"... impeding the processes by which the brain localizes a noxious stimulus can reduce pain, and that this effect reflects modulation of multimodal neural activities."*

Sometimes, all it takes to expedite a jump to a pain-free reality is taking a moment to give yourself a hug. Something special happens when your arms cross over the midline of your body. Iannetti and colleagues explain, *"Crossing the hands over the body midline impairs (the brain's) ability to localize tactile stimuli."*

Perform & Persevere Better by Crossing Your Arms

University of Rochester psychologists Ron Friedman and Andrew Elliot conducted the first experiments to test the hypothesis that people who cross their arms receive a proprioceptive cue to persevere, and that arm crossing leads to greater persistence on unsolvable anagram puzzles and improved performance on solvable anagrams. The idea here is that body language doesn't just communicate how we're feeling to others—it also has the power to influence our own behavior.

Friedman and Eliot informed participants that the purpose of this study was to test the effects of motor activity on analytical reasoning skills—specifically, any relationship between arm movement and analytical processing. They further explained they were testing whether or not arm movement helps this type of processing, and that the participant has been randomly assigned to the stationary arm group. Participants were then asked to either sit with their hands on the table, on their thighs, or in an arms crossed position while focusing on the puzzles at hand.

The researchers found their hypothesis was correct—arm crossing improves both puzzle-solving performance (when puzzles can actually be solved), and perseverance. Intriguingly, study participants appeared to be totally unaware of the effects of arm crossing on their puzzle solving, and their mood was not affected at all, even though their behavior was noticeably affected by crossing their arms. If people were getting some kind of proprioceptive cue to persevere, they certainly weren't aware of it.

Next time you find yourself facing a seemingly insolvable task or a situation of adversity where you'd love to achieve good results and your performance is key to your success, take a few minutes to cross your arms while thinking about your strategy, and precisely what things you'll need to do for success. Envision yourself easily handling each and every aspect required of you smoothly and gracefully, with excellent results. Visualize yourself achieving tremendous success while breathing deep, slow, regular breaths from your abdomen, down below your belly button.

Make a Fist or Stretch Fingers to Increase Willpower

When we make a clenched fist, we are adopting one of the most commonly recognized physical mannerisms of resolve. As it turns out, this simple movement has been experimentally found by psychologists to increase willpower. Rather than the old model described by Saint Augustine, *"The mind commands the body and it obeys,"* emerging research   now indicates that communication between the mind and body runs both ways. In the new model of Embodied Cognition, psychologists see evidence supporting the idea that the body exerts tremendous influence that shapes a person's thoughts and feelings.

Iris Hung from the National University of Singapore collaborated with Aparna Labroo of the University of Chicago to test their hypothesis that clenching one's fists and firming one's muscles can increase willpower and self-control. Hung and Labroo devised a series of five different studies designed to evaluate what effect fist-clenching (from tightly grasping a pen in their fists) had on: making donations to the Red Cross to benefit residents of earthquake-devastated Haiti, withstanding an uncomfortable position purportedly for better health (immersing one hand in a bucket of ice water), drinking something unpleasant (vinegar) purportedly for better health, and choosing healthier snacks.

These studies demonstrated remarkable evidence that simply firming one's muscles can firm one's resolve and facilitate self-control. Many different types of muscle-firming were part of these studies, including: fist-clenching, finger stretching, tightening calf muscles, and firming biceps. The researchers noted that *"firming muscles by clenching a fist does not make people 'tightfisted'; rather it helps them open their hearts and wallets for others."*

Any time you face situations that test your willpower, such as when you choose what to order at a restaurant, or whether to keep your commitment to your exercise or dietary plans, you can bolster your intentions to do what you know to be best by firming your muscles. You can even do this discreetly while sitting, by tensing the muscles in the calves of your legs, or stretching your fingers out wide while stretching, and these movements likely won't be misconstrued by people around you.

Skip to Increase Energy

Students in Dutch behavioral psychologist Erik Peper's holistic health class at San Francisco State University are used to a lot of ups and downs—as every half hour or so, Peper stops lecturing and asks the class to *"get up and wiggle."* Such seemingly nontraditional teaching methods may become the norm, when educators become familiar with some of Peper's more remarkable research findings.

Peper's body of work pays close attention to how simple changes in body posture influence mood and self-reported energy levels. One student in Peper's class remarked, *"My energy slowly drained and I became more sleepy the longer the lecture lasted; however, when the instructor guided us through a few physical movements, my energy and mood significantly increased. I can pay much more attention."*

One of the best ways to get a giant positive boost of energy that Peper and his research colleagues have found is to skip with

167

opposite arms and legs raised at the same time. Such "cross crawl skipping" feels happy and positive, and evokes happy childhood memories while dramatically boosting peoples' energy, whereas walking in a slouched posture leads study participants to feel sad, lonely, isolated, zombie-like and sleepy.

What I find most amazing about Peper's skipping research study is that the most depressed (bottom 20%) study participants felt just as energized after skipping as the least depressed (top 20%) people did after just two or three minutes of skipping in the hallways. I can personally attest to the positive energizing power of skipping, as it's something I've loved to do since I was a little girl, and I've never quite given it up. I consistently feel a dramatic boost in energy any time I skip, and evidently skipping is something that gives everyone who can do it quite a powerful positive energy boost. It's effects are remarkable for anyone, but are particularly dramatic for those who are feeling down or depressed.

Improve Relationships by Acting Close

University of Hertfordshire psychology professor Richard Wiseman may have begun his working life as a professional magician, but no amount of magic books could explain   the amazing results he got when he conducted an experiment with a hundred speed-daters in Edinburgh, Scotland. Wiseman separated the speed-daters into two groups: one which conducted the speed dating activities as usual, and the other with special instructions for couples to pretend they were already intimately acquainted. These couples were instructed to hold hands, share secrets, and gaze into each others' eyes.

At the end of the study when all the speed-daters were asked how close they felt to their partners, and how many of them would like to see their partners again, only about 20% of the conventional daters indicated a desire to reconnect, compared with 45% in the pretending-to-be-intimate group. Wiseman explains,

"The assumption was that the emotion leads to the action or behavior but this shows it can happen the other way around, action can lead to emotions. Behaving like you are in love can lead to actually falling in love."

Wiseman adds,

"Actions are the quickest, easiest, and most powerful way to instantly change how you think and feel."

University of California at San Diego psychology professor, Dr. Robert Epstein, conducted similar exercises, asking couples of students to participate in what he called "soul gazing"— looking deeply into each other's eyes. Epstein found a 7% increase in loving, an 11% increase in liking, and a 45% increase in closeness... with 89% of participants reporting the exercise increased feelings of intimacy.

Epstein's love-building exercises include embracing each other gently while sensing and synchronizing breathing, placing the palm of your hand as close as possible to your partner's palm without actually touching for several minutes (in which you might not only feel heat, but surprisingly also some sparks), write down secrets and discuss them, fall backward into the arms of your partner, mirror each others' movements, and try a mind-reading game.

Taking action to become closer to loved ones is not inauthentic, explains Dr. Epstein. It's something we can actively do to improve our relationships, rather than passively accepting the status quo.

"The students in my course were doing something new— taking control over their love lives. We grow up on fairy

tales and movies in which magical forces help people find their soul mates, with whom they effortlessly live happily ever after."

The fact that we can increase closeness by acting close in relationships is wonderful news for both old and new relationships. The findings from these studies give credence to the advice of our parents and grandparents who impressed upon us the importance of good social manners. When we make eye contact, shake hands, and inquire how others are doing rather than only talk about ourselves, we're well on our way to becoming a bit closer to people we might otherwise not care nearly so much about.

Boost Drug Efficacy by Watching Advertisements

One of the best things you can do once you're already taking some kind of pharmaceutical prescription or supplements is to view supportive advertisements for the treatment you're taking. Researchers conducted randomized clinical trials to see what impact, if any, direct-to-consumer advertisements might have on the efficacy of branded drugs. Study subjects watched a movie that was spliced with advertisements for Claritin or Zyrtec antihistamine treatments. Researchers noted that people who watched the Claritin advertisements found Claritin to be more effective, and concluded that branded drugs can interact with exposure to television advertisements.

You can create your own "advertisements" to boost efficacy of whatever you're doing for your betterment. Make a poem about your vitamins and post it on your refrigerator, set it to music and sing it every now and then... and see if you're feeling more energetic, mentally sharp, and healthy. Saying to people (or even just talking aloud to yourself) something like, "I'm

170

walking to get fit and trim," or "I'm eating fresh fruits and vegetables to feel healthier" can reinforce existing beliefs and improve your results with whatever steps you're already taking to make a quantum jump in your life.

Become Smarter by Pointing to Your Head

Psychologists Adam Fetterman and Michael Robinson of North Dakota State University conducted a study to determine just how much of a difference there is between those who focus on their heads more than their hearts. They confirmed that those who identify with their heads tended to be rational, logical, and more socially cold compared to those who identify with their hearts. These people tended to be more accurate when answering general knowledge questions, and had higher grade point averages.

Surprisingly, people who were randomly manipulated to move their non-dominant hand to point toward their heads enjoyed elevated test scores when answering general knowledge questions, compared to a control group whose individuals did not point toward their heads. The researchers hypothesized that drawing participants' attention to their head made them aware on some level of the rational stereotype associated with the head, which then influenced their behavior.

Since effects are noticeable within minutes of doing such a simple thing as pointing to your head, this is something you can do any time you need to think more clearly. You can point toward your head any time you're about to take an important test, make an influential presentation, or go for an interview, for example. This action is so simple and easy to do, and it requires no special equipment that you should definitely give it a try the next time you feel you could use a bit of an infusion of intellectual genius. This is something you can do a few minutes before you need the extra brainpower, so be sure to point to your head in private for best results, rather than during your presentation or interview!

Boost Emotional Intelligence by Pointing to Your Heart

Psychologists Adam Fetterman and Michael Robinson conducted a research study that found that those who identify with their hearts more than their heads tend to be more emotional, feminine, and interpersonally warm, and more likely to favor emotional over rational considerations when making moral or ethical decisions.

Intriguingly, study participants who were asked randomly to point toward their hearts improved their ability to make emotionally-centered decisions. The influence of such a subtle movement to make a noticeable difference is truly remarkable, and something we can all benefit from any time we feel a need for a boost in our social and emotional intelligence.

Are you having trouble understanding your sibling, parent, spouse or boss? Take a break for a few minutes and breathe deeply and slowly while placing your hand over your heart. Slow your breathing to the slowest, steadiest, deepest breathing rhythm that works well for you. Envision yourself feeling closer with the person you have in mind, and having a better understanding of how they feel, what matters most to them, and what you most need to know about them right now.

If you're gathering a group of people together who you'd like to be more emotionally sensitive, consider starting the meeting by playing the national anthem, and asking people to put their hands over their hearts for the duration of the song. You can try this out to see if people get along a little better with a few moments of placing their hands over their hearts.

Improve Your Vision by Changing Your Mindset

You might think that your visual acuity is something fixed and stationary that can't be influenced by your surroundings or how you're thinking... and you'd be wrong. Researchers led by Ellen Langer of Harvard University conducted a series of experiments that demonstrate it's not just a matter of how good your eyes are—your mindset has a tremendous powerful influence on your vision as well. Study participants who were informed that a given type of exercise—jumping jacks—would improve their vision were able to see much more clearly afterward than people doing a comparable and equally athletic activity—skipping. *"Many things that we think we can't do are a function of our mindset rather than our abilities to do them,"* Langer says.

Study participants given eye charts to read that were arranged in reverse order, with the smallest letters up at the top and increasingly larger letters going down, they saw letters in rows they could not see before. This may have been due to the fact that people expect to be able to read the top rows of letters on eye charts, so they are able to even when the eye chart row sequence is reversed, or the letters on the eye chart are smaller than usual.

Another one of Langer's ingenious experiments involved testing people's vision who wore pilot's uniforms and sat in flight simulators. These people scored a whopping 40% better on vision tests than a control group of ROTC students placed in similar conditions, but with a "broken" simulator who just pretended to fly a plane. Apparently people have such strong learned associations that pilots have excellent vision that they are able to transfer the expected benefits of being a pilot to their own vision.

These visual experiments demonstrate that our mindset plays a powerful role in our visual acuity. The Bates Method of visual improvement depends upon this basic principle. Some of the Bates Method's practitioners, such as Meir Schneider. Meir Schneider cured himself of congenital blindness as a teenager, and now has a California driver's license and informs people that they don't need to wear eyeglasses. Schneider teaches people to improve their vision without wearing eyeglasses through a series of exercises including one in which people say aloud while gazing at black text on a white page, *"The words are black, the page is white."* Amazingly, such a simple psychological exercise really does make a profound positive difference in vision in a relatively short period of time.

*   *   *

The next chapter, Chapter Six, *Quantum Jumps in Daily Life,* is designed to help you take some ideas that are most pertinent and relevant for you, and prepare you to make full use of them in your life. You might want to have a pen or pencil and some paper ready to jot down some notes!

Exercise:

Fake a Smile for Greater Happiness

Put a pen between your teeth for a few minutes, and observe if the world seems transformed into a slightly happier place. Force a smile, showing your teeth and curling the edges of your mouth upward. If this seems silly and you're able to, laugh for no reason at all. Don't worry what your laugh and smile look and sound like— all that counts is making the effort at all. You'll get positive benefits from just doing your best. Crinkle up your eyes, raise your cheeks and enjoy the health benefits of reduced stress, released endorphins, and an overall calmer, happier disposition from smiling for no reason at all. Once you've done this exercise, read or watch something funny, and laugh... even if you don't at first find anything amusing. Just working your laugh and smile muscles is doing you a world of good.

Exercise:

Write What Went Well Today

Write down three good things that happened in the past twenty-four hours, leaving space underneath each entry to write a couple more sentences. Starting with the first thing that went well in the past day, ask yourself what you had to do with this good experience and write that down under each of the three things that went well during the past twenty-four hours. Be especially mindful to credit yourself for setting a good example for others in the world if part of the reason good things have happened is thanks to your qualities of: Gratitude, Love, Kindness, Honesty, Bravery, Creativity, Hope, Zest, or Perseverance. Feeling better attuned to what matters most helps you feel truly prosperous, based on what's going well right now in your life.

Exercise:

Soul Gazing for Better Relationships

For this exercise you need a partner who is willing to do the exercise with you. Start by sitting comfortably facing one another, preferably at a distance of two to three feet apart. Set a timer for at least two minutes, and up to five minutes time. Look deeply into one another's eyes quietly, without talking, for at least two minutes. As you are looking into each others' eyes, imagine you are gazing into the very core of your beings. Talk with your partner about what you saw and felt.

Exercise:

Sharing Secrets for Better Relationships

For this exercise you need a partner who is willing to do the exercise with you. Answer the following questions one at a time on separate pieces of paper, so you and your partner each have a pile of folded papers with one secret each written on them, that you can trade one at a time. Here are some questions for each of you to answer: What is something you've long wanted to do that you haven't done yet? What do you love best about your best friend? When's the last time you laughed so hard it hurt? What advice would you give your ten-year-old self? If you had a time machine, when (and where) would you visit? What's your favorite superpower?

Exercise:

Envision Positive Aging Stereotypes

When you think of old people, what are the five most positive words or phrases that come to mind? Write down the names of senior citizens who are strong, witty, vibrant, and wise. Write down five positive words or phrases you'd like to embody as you grow older. Close your eyes and imagine your best possible senior future self... and notice what this positive example of growing old has to teach you that you can start doing for better emotional, physical, and mental health right now.

Exercise:

Strike Some Power Poses for Greater Confidence

Try out every expansive pose, and hold each one for anywhere from a few seconds to a few minutes at a time. Lean back in a chair with your hands clasped behind your head. Stretch one hand off to the side, and rest it on whatever's nearby (such as another chair). Sit at your desk and kick your feet up on the top of your desk. When you stand up, lean forward with both hands palm-down. Stand up and place your hands on your hips. Notice how you're feeling now.

Exercise:

Act Extroverted for Greater Happiness

Next time you are in a social setting, go out of your way to meet and greet other people, shake hands if and when appropriate, and ask them how they're doing. Smile, maintain eye contact, and do your best to respond appropriately as they respond.

*"Any man who can hitch the length and
breadth of the galaxy, rough it, slum it,
struggle against terrible odds, win
through, and still know where his towel
is, is clearly a man to be reckoned with."*

—*Douglas Adams*

Chapter 6

Quantum Jumps in

Daily Life

What would make you truly happy?

My mother used to ask my sister and I this question when we were growing up, and over the years I've increasingly come to appreciate the wonderfully transformative effect it's had on the way I think and view the world. I've noticed, for example, that it's almost impossible for me to stay in a grumpy mood or regularly complain about what's going wrong and what's most unfair in the world when someone asks me and shows they genuinely want to know, *"What would make you truly happy?"*

Without over-thinking the question, take a moment right now to write down the first thoughts that come to mind about what would truly bring you joy right here, right now. Write down things that matter most to *you*, rather than what you think other people would expect you to say. This exercise works best when you refrain from judging what comes to mind, being open and accepting of whatever thoughts come forth. If taking a nap would truly make you happy right now, be honest with yourself and add it to your list.

Close your eyes and visualize yourself having an experience with someone or something that would make you truly happy. In your mind's eye, look around this imagined reality, paying close attention to how you look and behave in this idyllic scene. Appreciate how good it feels to enjoy all the perks and benefits of this reality, and ask for intuitive inspiration and insights to help you reach this goal. When you open your eyes, tell yourself,

"I now have everything I need, and
I know exactly what to be and do."

Just as most parents wish their children will love and be loved, follow their dreams, find success and be happy—we also wish all these things for ourselves at some level. Most of us can at least think of enjoyable realities we'd wish for ourselves on a mental level. It may take a bit of imagination practice to become good at feeling we truly deserve good things, holding a clear vision of being able to enjoy them with blessings from friends, colleagues, family, and others wishing us well and helping ensure our abundant success and prosperity.

The big question is, with so many possible areas we can benefit from with quantum jumping, where do we start, and how can we know what is really possible?

Envision Future Memories

If you've ever daydreamed, you've likely had future memories—a sense of having already experienced something before you actually have. Future memories are terrific guideposts for helping us envision and select between parallel possible realities even as they are beginning to unfold before us, inviting us to walk forward as if they are red carpets rolling out toward us at this decision point right here, right now. When we have future memories of possible futures, we gain the benefit of making changes that can either bring us into or take us away from the possible futures we've seen.

Sometimes when we notice a feeling of déjà vu, we recognize we've previously dreamed of exactly what is unfolding in this very moment. In such moments, an interweaving between the world of dreams and daily life comes through, along with a sense that on a very deep level, everyday life is constantly guided by our dreams. There is a gift both in seeing a future memory, and in noting whether it points in a direction we wish to pursue. There is also a gift in recognizing a previous premonition in which we see something wonderful we've previously known only in dreams.

If we get a glimpse, for example, of a possible reality in which our luggage has been stolen... or in which we find a beautiful ring in a consignment shop... and we sense we've seen these possible futures before, we can decide whether or not we'd like to visit these other realities or possible futures. Both of these future memories came through to me when I was traveling through southern California, and despite one premonition seeming to be bad news, both turned out to be very helpful.

When I first saw a beautiful diamond and garnet reversible ring in a Santa Barbara consignment shop, it looked so familiar to me that I knew at first glance it was one I knew quite well, despite the fact that I'd never before held or tried on any kind of reversible ring before. I recognized my familiarity with what ought to have been a very unfamiliar piece of jewelry as having come from a prior future memory, and heeded the good feelings I got from holding it as a positive sign that this ring was meant for me. In a sense I got the benefit of both looking forward to enjoying this ring at some point in the future when I first daydreamed about it, and then I got to savor it when I could hold it for real in my hands in Santa Barbara. This is a lot like looking forward to a special occasion or event and then enjoying it again when the big day actually arrives—I get to enjoy it twice as much!

My second future memory experience on that same southern California trip occurred in Los Angeles when I was talking with friends at brunch one morning. I suddenly received an awareness that I was viewing a possible future in which all of our luggage was stolen while we were away, because thieves came through after we left our luggage in the room. This future memory even included visualization of how my friend would cheer me with kind words after the theft, reassuring me that we still had our health and each other, and were unharmed. I told my friends of this fleeting possible future memory, and we agreed to take our luggage with us.

It's inspiring to read real life accounts from people who've made quantum jumps in their lives, and it's also inspiring to remember times in your life that you've made quantum jumps before, too. Just as with any new skill, it's important to give yourself sufficient time to make quantum jumping a more conscious process, and not give up simply because progress can sometimes seem slow. The most important thing to practice with respect to quantum jumping is mindfulness—getting and staying aware of your thoughts and feelings in a compassionate, non-judgmental state of awareness.

Make a Commitment to Achieving Excellence

During a particularly grueling series of practice kicks, my martial arts instructor once asked our class, *"Do you know when most people quit?"* He then drew a curve that started off with a gentle slope on the left, as he explained, *"When people first start learning something new, they often feel they are making progress fairly rapidly. After a while, they feel a plateau."* He drew a mostly flat area up high toward the right. *"This is the point where most people give up, thinking they can't improve any more... right before they would have gotten their black belt, for example."*

For many of us, progress is most clearly evident when we first learn something new. As we keep learning, we can sometimes get bored with continuing the necessary practice required to make our next leaps onward and upward to genuine improvement... yet such practice makes a big difference. We usually know exactly what we need to be doing in order to be enjoying the benefits of the life we wish to live; we need to make a commitment to ourselves to follow through and do what we need to be doing to be living that life of our dreams.

Quantum jumping requires commitment. Most people feel excited when first envisioning new realities, and it's easy to feel enthusiasm in the early stages of trying something new. Some of the ideas in the previous chapter show simple things you can do to start moving forward right now toward living a happier, more prosperous life, yet they are just the first steps—the starting points. To maintain momentum you'll need to make a commitment to yourself to achieve excellence by setting personal goals, and doing what you know needs to be done.

Meditate to Develop Mindfulness

In order to experience continuing success with quantum jumps, it's absolutely necessary to keep your internal energy, or Qi, up. There are many ways you can work with your inner energy, such as practicing yoga, martial arts, or meditation. While each method and path is different, they can all be quite effective at giving you a sense of inner peace, harmony, balance and strength.

While you may have heard of some of the astonishing benefits lifelong meditators such as yogis gain, in terms of being

183

able to control things such as their breathing, body temperature and heart rate... did you know that novice meditators who'd never meditated before in their lives can experience such profound changes in their brains that it shows up after just two months of meditation practice? Medical researchers in Massachusetts affiliated with Harvard Medical School and Massachusetts General Hospital found that meditation enhanced areas of the brains of meditation-naïve study participants within the left hippocampus portion of their brains. This indicates that mindfulness-based meditation is associated with changes in gray matter concentration in the regions of the brain involved with learning and memory processes, emotion regulation, self-referential processing and perspective-taking.

Practicing meditation on a daily basis even for just a few minutes a day makes a huge difference in quantum jumping results. After many months of daily meditation, you may think nothing is happening, and that you might as well quit. This is the point where it's good to remember the plateau and realize there is a place where while it seems nothing is happening, big changes are about to occur! Consider that most changes take place beneath our current conscious perceptual awareness— barely discernible to you, but quite evident to the multiverse of possibilities.

The more we meditate and practice meditative energy exercises on a daily basis such as yoga, Tai Chi, or martial arts— which all require us to practice focusing our breath, movement and intention together as one—the more we move our "set point" of recognizing and accepting that everything right here, right now is well. Such practices allow us access to our inner "observer"—that part of us that is pure awareness and quite impervious to all the ups and downs our ego personalities regularly face. The following two steps absolutely transform us in ways that ensure that overall, we won't hit emotional or energetic lows anywhere near as low as we've previously encountered:

(1) Develop a breath, movement, and intention practice long enough to

(2) Realize there is a part of us that is connected to the eternal infinite.

Starting and maintaining a daily practice of meditation is one of the best things you can do for yourself, since this is one of the most effective available tools for keeping yourself focused on good news. It can be easy to look down at a puddle in a pothole in the road ahead of us, yet when we are driving a motorcycle. we must learn to keep our eyes fixed on the horizon, rather than staring down in order that we miss the pothole and arrive safely at our destination. The pothole will still be visible to us in our peripheral vision, but there's no need for us to actually hit it and end up flying off our motorbike.

One of the greatest gifts of meditation is the power it gives us to see ourselves in a fresh, new light. Rather than thinking of ourselves as limited to being who we or others think we are, we slowly gain a deep sense of being something much greater than we could ever fully explain or describe. We can touch a sense of eternity—of timelessness—and a feeling of being able to observe ourselves in our bodies with our emotions, and actions and words. This is an experience of ourselves as consciousness, which is free from fear, and capable of great patience, kindness, and love. This is an experience of seeing a vast range of options ever opening before us, from which we are so very blessed and fortunate to be able to choose. When we are aware of identifying with ourselves as embodied consciousness continuously selecting which material reality we choose to experience, it's easier to keep our energy up to a high enough vibration to hold fast a vision of how truly good life can be.

The best times of day to meditate are any time you have the time and focus to do it. If you have a quiet time to yourself in the morning or at night, make use of it to meditate. Your health and peace of mind will benefit tremendously when you find ways to fit your meditation practice into your daily life, so it becomes a regular part of your day.

Some people meditate upon awakening, and some when they go to bed. Others make time before or after meals, or associated with daily commutes or drives (exercising caution when driving). Some people meditate while walking, some while gardening, some while doing dishes, and some while humming or playing music. When you find the kind of meditation mindfulness practice that works best for you, you'll be more likely to stick with it until you start noticing positive effects.

Create Your Own Customized Meditation

Have you ever wished you could meditate, but felt meditation is somehow beyond you? Meditation doesn't necessarily require sitting for long hours in lotus position while breathing first through one nostril and then through the other, chanting "Om." You can create your own type of meditation custom-fitted to who you are, based on combining a favorite way of relaxing with one of your favorite ways to focus your attention. Not only will you get the benefits from meditation that sometimes take a while for you to consciously recognize, but you'll have a good time doing it!

When you think about your favorite ways to relax, consider some of the most soothing activities people enjoy, such as: listening to music, gardening, resting in a hammock, taking a
186

hot bath, or going for a walk. When you pick something you can do year-round, you'll be more likely to keep your meditation practice going, so if your first choice is weather-dependent, such as gardening, pick something you can do at any time of year.

A favorite focus of attention might include something like: paying attention to your breathing, observing your thoughts, repeating a mantra (a special word or phrase), feeling your internal energy flow, feeling the touch of the tip of your thumbs to the tip of your pinky finger, or clearing your mind of stray thoughts. You'll know your choice of focus is perfect when it brings your attention to this present place and time, right here, right now.

Now the fun begins! You can create your very own customized meditation by putting together one or more of your favorite activities with one or more of your favorite ways to focus your attention. You can try slowing down your breathing while taking a bath, or repeating a mantra while taking a walk. You don't need to limit yourself only to ideas mentioned here—this is a great time to be creative. Ask yourself what you do that relaxes you most, and try out different ways of focusing your attention to see what works best for you. Make sure you practice your meditation for at least a few minutes each day, and pay attention to how you feel after a few days or weeks of regular meditation.

Be More Agreeable for Greater Contentment

Have you ever thought that if only you had a different job, a different spouse, or lived in a different location you'd be a whole lot happier? While that might be true to some degree, recent research shows such external circumstances only contribute about 10% to peoples' overall happiness. About half of our overall happiness is attributable to nature, or what we inherited from our parents, leaving roughly a rather sizable 40% of our happiness to be determined by the activities we choose to engage in.

Researchers at the University of Manchester in England studied 8,625 people between the ages of 15 and 93 at two points in time, four years apart, and found that small shifts in personality were more closely tied to life satisfaction than any other indicators. Examples of such shifts in personality are things like becoming more agreeable, or more open—both of which contributed more to increased contentment than changing demographic factors such as marital status and employment. Christopher Boyce and his colleagues in Manchester note, *"Personality has also been shown to predict the well-being response following important life events such as unemployment, disability, widowhood, and income increases."*

When personality is considered as an independent variable on par with other 'variable' economic factors, researchers are finding that changes in a person's 'big five' dimensions of a personality (openness-to-experience, conscientiousness, extroversion, agreeableness, and neuroticism) are some of the best indicators of life satisfaction over time.

"Not only does personality change occur, but it is an important influence and a possible route to greater well-being," research psychologist Christopher Boyce now of the University of Stirling in Scotland remarked.

The more experienced we are, the easier it is for us to say, *"I know that"* upon encountering something familiar. We feel delighted to recognize a familiar concept, and are quite happy to find confirmation of our beliefs. The problem with stopping at this point and categorizing new experiences in terms of something familiar is that we risk completely missing out on the unexpected... the unanticipated... the surprising... the amazingly, astonishingly new.

If we look and listen a little more carefully, we can release ourselves from the constraints of predetermined judgment, and open ourselves up to expanded awareness of multiple coexisting harmonious meanings. As soon as we stop our questioning process, we essentially imprison ourselves in whatever set of beliefs we happen to be holding onto at that moment. Fortunately, there's hope for all of us, including even the most curmudgeonly know-it-alls.

Be Open to New Experience & Stay Mentally Sharp

We often expect that as we age, we inevitably experience a whole host of declining social, physical and psychological skills, but recent studies show this need not be the case. Psychologist Joshua Jackson and his research associates found that even "older dogs" can learn new tricks... and they've discovered that we can increase one of the big five components of personality that we've just recently learned can be changed over time. Their research participants included 183 older adults ranging in age from 60 to 94 years in a Midwestern American city. These senior citizens received instruction in a 16 week home-based inductive reasoning training program to complete crossword and Sudoku puzzles. Recruitment materials for this study indicated that the program, Senior Odyssey, was a 'fun and engaging program studying ways to prevent mental decline including memory loss.'

This study found that the participants made noticeable positive changes in their openness to new experiences, such as learning how to do a new kind of puzzle. A benefit from this openness was indeed increased mental acuity, but more amazingly, this study was one of the first to conclusively demonstrate that personality traits *can* change through non-psychopharmacological interventions, and are not fixed for most or all of our lives. Openness is a particularly wonderful personality trait to improve, since it's predictive of better health and longer life. One of the best things about this study is that seniors continued increasing in openness both during and after the study ended—indicating authentic changes were obtained.

Focus on Good News, Keep Bad News at Periphery

One of the best things to remember is that life is not so much what happens to you, but rather how you respond to inevitable ups and downs along the way. An excellent living example demonstrating the point that what we focus on becomes who we are is the Dalai Lama. If we were to review the facts about how he's been driven from his Tibetan homeland,

190

with friends and family killed and treated terribly, we might expect that he would be a bitter person, understandably focused on how best to retaliate against aggressors and oppressors and how to exact revenge or some kind of justice. Thanks to his daily practice of meditation and steady focus on what matters most— a religion based on kindness and compassion—the reality is that the Dalai Lama is one of the most upbeat, friendly, positive, joyful people you could hope to meet on our planet.

Such optimism is clearly an asset, as researchers have found that optimists are less likely to give up when the going gets tough, and more likely to plan a successful course of action with help from others, all the while staying focused on finding solutions. Even when it seems nothing at all has gone well, optimists look for—and find—"existential resources." Dr. Suzanne Segerstrom, professor of psychology at the University of Kentucky, explains that we can find important ways to grow in a positive way when life brings us proverbial lemons. Dr. Segerstrom mentions some emotion-focused strategies optimists employ when facing uncontrollable stressors, such as, *"I look for something good in what is happening," "I try to see it in a different light, to make it seem more positive,"* and *"I came out of the experience better than when I went in."*

Dr. Segerstrom believes even pessimists can learn to become optimists, and she recommends the best way to make this particular leap is to fake optimism until you actually become optimistic. One way to face optimism is to pursue goals... and Dr. Segerstrom recommends some types of goals over others, as well as choosing your own goals rather than adopting goals someone has set for you. Segerstrom explains,

> *"In general, people are happier when pursuing goals that help them grow as people, have meaningful relationships, and contribute to society, and they are less happy when*

they're pursuing goals that help them be more attractive, rich, popular, or famous."

Keeping a positive, optimistic focus when seeing or hearing news requires concentration, since most news as reported in the mainstream media emphasizes emotionally disturbing events, from the "if it bleeds, it leads" mindset. While upsetting news may sell newspapers, it does little for improving the quality of our lives. Fortunately, there is a way to acknowledge 'bad' news in such a way that we allow it the opportunity to transform: we keep it at the periphery of awareness. In much the same way that spoons are most likely to bend when not being stared at, reality most often shifts for people and things at the periphery of our awareness, right at the edge of what we're most intently observing.

What I recommend doing when seeing "bad" news is to keep it as far to the edge of your thoughts as possible. In other words, if you see something that falls under the category of 'bad news' online, resist the temptation to forward or share it. If someone emails it to you, briefly skim through the message before archiving or deleting it. Keep everything that's emotionally disturbing off to the periphery of your mind's eye, where you can see potential problems coming if anything starts to become a direct threat to you or those you love, without such sharp focus of attention that you're 'locking it in' to any of your possible realities.

In keeping with getting and maintaining a more positive focus of attention, when so inspired, distract yourself away from dwelling on 'bad' news by actively seeking out 'good news' items relevant to what you are doing and goals you are working toward, and showing historical trends you'd love to see come into prominence and popularity. What you will find is that over time, good news will start overwhelming the bad. This is a wonderful way to assist so-called "impossible causes," by focusing on what we're grateful for until increasing numbers of other people are similarly intrigued and focused on these good things, too.

If you have a hard time staying focused on the positive aspects in life because you keep thinking about what might go wrong, you're in luck. Researchers have been making progress finding a number of proven ways to reduce fears, and at least one of them is bound to help you.

Journal & Exercise to Overcome Anxiety & Fear

Any time you've ever choked up or procrastinated instead of achieving a goal, you've come face-to-face with the debilitating effect fear can have in our lives. Researchers have found that there is hope for the fearful and anxious, and there are tools we can use to improve our performance while removing interference. As Australian sports psychologist Dr. Craig Manning puts it, the recipe for high performance consists of "... *potential plus training minus interference.*" The interference Dr. Manning is talking about consists of any guilt over perceived mistakes from the past, as well as fear about possible problems in the future. While most of us recognize the importance of intrinsic potential, and many of us are willing to work hard to improve, the key aspect of interference is seldom properly addressed. Clearly, this factor is essential to deal with, since many people who are obviously gifted, talented and motivated don't make it to the pinnacle of success in their fields.

Dr. Manning explains that one of the best things you can do to ensure success is focus your energy and attention on what you *can* control right now, rather than what you can't. Such clear focus on what you *can* do that you are responsible for prevents you from losing energy fretting over things beyond your control. High-performing people are good at staying almost exclusively focused on what they are responsible for and what they can do right here, right now. High-performers work hard perfecting their skills and completing tasks. Their example inspires others, as they do their best and work hard to improve wherever possible. High-performers attune their minds with their spiritual side—that part of consciousness that feels timeless, expansive, and fearless—so they can channel emotions in constructive ways and communicate effectively with others and the world around them. High-performing individuals are highly motivated, confident, decisive, focused, and have low levels of anxiety... and every one of these qualities can be developed and improved.

University of Chicago psychology professor, Sian Beilock, offers additional assistance in removing fear-based interference. Beilock studies how to avoid 'choking' when facing stressful situations so we can perform better under the inevitable pressures we face in life. Beilock recommends writing down feelings of concern prior to stressful events, since studies show that getting feelings of anxiety off one's chest makes a huge positive difference in results: *"... students who wrote for ten minutes about their worries before the math test performed roughly 15% better than the students who sat and did nothing before the exam."* Beilock theorizes that writing down one's concerns is helpful because it pulls us out of worrying and ruminating into focusing on something we *can* do—writing down how we feel—in a way that helps us reassess our emotions and reframe ourselves in a more positive position relative to the situation at hand.

An additional anti-anxiety tip from Beilock has to do with conscious and unconscious stereotypes of ourselves and how we feel people of our age, race, gender and other attributes tend to do in what we're about to undertake. Research findings are showing that we are much more affected by stereotypes than most of us ever realize. When facing pressure to perform in a situation with high stakes, studies show it's best to ignore or actively discount any negative stereotypes you might have heard that could place you in a group that's not expected to succeed. I suggest getting proactive with this, so before going into such situations, tell yourself that there are outstanding successful people very much like you who do brilliantly well in this kind of situation.

I employed this approach while taking advanced math classes in high school. I was the only girl who frequently outscored the all-male members of our school's competitive "Mathletes" team, and I sensed a great deal of stereotypical surprise and consternation from repeatedly doing so well in my advanced math classes, I kept telling myself, *"There are lots of girls like me who do well in math and science."* I kept telling myself this all the way through my college years at UC Berkeley, where I majored in Physics and was one of just a handful of young women in the Physics graduating class. I'm absolutely certain that my positive mindset of actively countering stereotypes such as "women don't excel at math and major in Physics" helped ensure my success.

Yet another excellent way to reduce fear and anxiety is to exercise. While not a quick fix, this longer-term strategy takes at least a month to start taking effect... so once you start an exercise regimen you enjoy, don't quit. Michael Hopkins of the Neurobiology of Learning and Memory Laboratory at Dartmouth reports, *"It looks more and more like the positive stress of exercise prepares cells and structures and pathways within the brain so that they're more equipped to handle stress in other forms."* This means the stress you get from pushing yourself to your physical limits can translate to improved resilience when facing psychological and emotional stressors in the rest of your life.

Meditate & Refocus to Manage Anger

You've likely heard advice when people feel anger to "Let it out," or "Don't hold it all in." The old thinking went that if anger is left inside you, it might fester and spread until the dark thoughts come out explosively later on. For this reason, people are often advised to pound or scream into a pillow, squeeze a stress ball until it's eyes bulge out, or go to the gym and hit the punching bag. In this pressure-cooker model of anger and catharsis, unvented anger can build up like steam to a point where the pressure-cooker can explode. Now it's time to forget all that, and learn to find more effective ways to manage anger.

Recent psychological studies show that contrary to popular belief, ranting and venting aren't the best ways to release anger. Decades of research are now showing a clear picture of how venting actually makes anger worse, whereas expressing anger in constructive, non-aggressive ways can be beneficial. Two such studies were conducted by researchers at the University of Wisconsin in Green Bay. These researchers surveyed rant website visitors, finding that although these ranters became relaxed immediately after posting, they also experienced more anger than most, scoring quite high on trait anger—a rating of how anger-prone a person is in general—and frequently expressed anger in maladaptive ways, such as damaged relationships, property damage, dangerous driving, and verbal and physical fights. Almost half of these rant-site visitors surveyed said that someone had told them they have anger problems, and over a third admitted they agreed that they do have a problem dealing with anger. A second part of this study found that most participants experienced negative mood shifts after reading rants, and also after writing rants of their own.

Numerous studies indicate that it's inadvisable to write rants, read rants, or otherwise vent anger by hitting pillows or doing anything that increases anger levels. All types of ramping

196

up anger through "venting" not only have been found to actually increase anger and decrease happiness, but they have been found to increase subsequent aggressive behavior as well. As it turns out, studies show people will far more effectively reduce anger by doing nothing at all for two minutes rather than punching a sand bag for as long as they want. Psychologist Brad Bushman conducted a series of fascinating studies at Iowa State. Study participants wrote essays which were then marked with *"This is one of the worst essays I have ever read!"* written on it, and later informed they had the opportunity to compete against the person who graded their essay, and if they won the game they had a choice of setting the volume of a blast of horrible noise at their opponent from anywhere between rather quiet all the way up to 105 decibels—roughly equivalent to a chain saw, pneumatic drill or jackhammer. Bushman's studies showed that those who did nothing at all for two minutes exhibited far less subsequent aggressive behavior even than those who distracted themselves by thinking about becoming physically fit... so there seems to be some advantage to meditating in a state of "no thought" for even as short a time as just two minutes.

A team of researchers found that certain kinds of writing about anger other than ranting exclusively about how bad the perceived source of anger is can be beneficial. This helpful kind of writing encourages people to focus on themselves rather than dwell so much on someone or something they are angry with. Whereas writing about who we are angry with leads to increased aggression, refocusing our thoughts and feelings back on ourselves can lead to insights, appreciation, and emotional growth. People who had been experiencing chronic pain and who wrote about their own feelings, thoughts and ideas, were able to find a kind of meaning behind their discomfort in doing this type of journaling.

Next time you get angry, remember that a "no thought" meditation, or writing in a journal about yourself and your plans and your feelings has the power to help manage anger much more effectively than blowing off steam. Jump into a reality of calm mindedness, and jump off the emotional merry-go-round of identifying with being a victim, perpetrator, or rescuer. Refocus your mind away from what triggers your anger, and you'll be far better positioned to move onward and upward to better realities in your life.

Quantum Jumps with Money

There are energies and emotions associated with money that deserve special recognition before visualizing achieving more money in your life. Just as your core beliefs about work, vacations, health and relationships have a lot to do with how well these areas tend to go for you, so too do your beliefs about money influence how you find, keep, and grow money in your life. It's possible to listen to and clear up internal conflicts you may have with money, and this process starts by learning to discern internal resistance by noticing where in your body any tension or tightness might be at times when you are meditating and relaxing. Your relationship with money is vitally important to your success bringing more of it into your life, just as your relationship with work or your health make a big difference in how well those things go for you.

To make quantum jumps to a life with more money, follow these three basic steps:

(1) Hold a vision of being prosperous

(2) Feel excited about your financial dreams coming true

(3) Take physical action to find, keep and grow money

The step about feeling genuinely excited is very important for quantum jumping with money, as it provides the energetic bridge into your desired reality. You can get into this enthusiastic state by remembering how you felt excited when looking forward to making a big change in your life when your life took a big turn for the better. This emotional feeling of buzzing with excitement and feeling so much happy anticipation you can barely stand it is wonderfully important, as is holding an image of your prosperity.

Quantum jumping with money is a lot like daydreaming about being rich one day, but with a real sense of enthusiasm and fun, and an openness to take steps and do things as they come to you.

If instead of feeling happy and excited, you notice tension or stress, listen to these feelings and write down whatever mental messages are associated with them. Chances are such feelings are providing you with clues as to some self-talk you've internalized that is feeling at odds with increased financial prosperity in your life. By writing down any of these beliefs, you can see what kinds of thoughts are running through your mind, and if they are not helping you stay positive, you can flip them around to their opposites to create your own personalized affirmations. Write these down where you can see them and read them aloud to yourself often, and you'll find it a great deal easier to quantum jump into a reality of financial prosperity.

Quantum Jump Out of Injury

One of the best times to remember you can make a quantum jump is immediately following an accident or injury. If ever there was an occasion when most of us would love access to an alternate history, this is the time! The important thing to think of any time you're involved in an accident or injury is that you've heard reports from people who have jumped to safety. Remember that people have made leaps from a reality in which they had a broken bone, for example, to a reality in which they were just bruised.

One approach that many people have success with is that next time you have an accident, such as shutting a door on your finger or burning your hand touching something hot, repeat the exact same motions that led up to the injury—with the exception that this time, you are omitting the action that caused the injury. Repeat these motions over and over and over again— dozens of times—until this newly revised version of reality in which everything went smoothly with no problem is believable to you.

Another approach many people have had wonderful results with is to place one or both hands over the area of injury while feeling love for the injured area and person, and visualizing the body part(s) and person in perfect health. Keep your hand or hands in position while breathing deep, full, steady breaths and visualizing that healing energy is running through your body out from your hands and to the area in need of healing.

Jump to a Reality Where You Find Lost Things

One of the more enjoyable ways to experience quantum jumps is to find yourself in a reality in which you're reunited with a favorite missing possession. You can start with the usual steps we typically follow when searching for something we've lost, that include:

(1) Retrace your steps to where the item was last seen and where it may have traveled,

(2) Ask anyone nearby if they've seen it,

(3) Ask the item to show itself by asking a question my mother taught me when I was very young, *"Now if I were* _____*(missing object), where would I hide?"*

(4) Tidy things up while searching. Put things together that are similar, creating a systematic process of elimination that makes it easier to spot the missing item later on.

After you've covered these search basics, it's time to harness the natural search powers of our brain. Researchers at UC Berkeley have found that your brain calls in backup to find lost things. We typically organize objects into one of one thousand categories in our mind, in such a way that when we see something, we can assign it to a logical and easily retrievable location in memory. While this may not in itself be all that remarkable, recent neuroscience studies show that when study participants are asked to look for something in particular, such as a person, their brains can be seen to widen the net of possible categories:

> *"... their brains also commandeered the brain regions responsible for perception of animals, body parts, action verbs and natural minerals and shifted them toward the perception of people. Likewise, when participants were seeking vehicles, the categories of tools, devices and structures were also stimulated by representations of vehicles."*

If after trying all the above steps, you still can't locate your missing item, it's time to pull out all the stops and resort to some really amazing natural quantum processes. Just as scientists are now discovering that plants try all possible pathways in order to maximize efficiency of light absorption in cells by virtue of a process called quantum coherence, so too can we take advantage of the fact that as many physicists believe, we and every object around us exists in a superposition of states.

When seeking lost keys, for example, envision there is more than one reality in which your keys exist. In some realities, your keys seem to be gone, and in others your keys are nearby in a perfectly accessible place. You are now seeking one of many possible realities in which your keys return to you. Without getting overly concerned with which particular realities have your keys and which don't, it's best to adopt the attitude seen in many a "Missing" poster that states, "No questions asked." In the realm of quantum physics, in which Shrödinger's cat is either alive or dead, we don't so much care about the details as to which of many possible realities the keys come back from, as long as they do return.

Once you've focused attention on what you're seeking, so as to expand your ability to find it with more of your brainpower actively being put to work, it's time to lighten your mood a little... and relax. Saying *"Hope for reality shift!"* the way my daughters did when they were young is an excellent way to feel a bit more light-spirited, thereby making it easier for you to make a jump between parallel worlds of possibility. What this phrase lacks in sophistication it more than compensates in successful returns of missing things—often either in places already thoroughly checked, or rather unexpected locations one would not expect (such as my toddler's favorite juice cup suddenly perched atop the refrigerator, or water shoes resting atop my daughter's pillow, or my favorite jewelry tucked inside a dresser drawer).

When lost objects reappear, they often seem a little shy... preferring to quietly sneak into an out-of-the-way location, rather than startling people by exuberantly popping into existence right before their very eyes. Trust your intuition, and look in even some of the strangest, least likely locations that come to mind. You might just be surprised to find what you've been looking for!

Intend to Become the Ultimate You

Thinking about ideas presented in this book from quantum biology, the placebo effect, and evidence of alternate histories, it's clear there is a growing body of evidence indicating that we're jumping between parallel worlds. If some of these ideas were completely new to you when you first started reading this book, you've hopefully become familiar enough with the concept of quantum jumps to by now enjoyed at least a few first-hand quantum jumping experiences.

Your present intentions can help find future potential outcomes that can pull you toward those favorable future realities. As many scientists recognize, a growing body of research in the field of retrocausality and bicausality indicates our usual view of cause-and-effect may be time-reversed. Such "backward causation" is part of the symmetry in nature, and helps explain how plants make use of quantum physics to find the most efficient pathways by which to convert photons from sunshine into energy.

Due to the way reality is not so much continuous as it is discrete, like frames in a movie, your consciousness has the ability to travel to many possible worlds, seldom noticing that you've traveled at all. As you move from frame to frame, you don't notice your consciousness just blipped away to pure energy and back to the (possibly quite new-to-you) reality that you now physically occupy, nor do you often notice that you've moved from one universe of possibility to another. The other people in your life are similarly seldom consciously aware of parallel universes of possibility, nor the reality that their consciousness awareness is blipping in and out of existence.

The reason it matters so much to be honest with yourself about your true desires is that's what you truly care about all the way through every fiber of your being. Knowing the difference between something you genuinely love and care about and something others tell you is supposed to be precious to you is important, and getting and staying focused on goals related to what you love most that relate to making yourself the best you can be is vitally important. Such focused, fully-aligned desires come forth into reality most readily. When you start with an intention such as, "How good can it get?" you won't waste time finding out that what you thought you wanted isn't actually all that enjoyable after all... and you'll enjoy every step of the journey of discovery.

Harness the Placebo Effect When Sick

Do you remember a time when after having been sick for a while, even though you still had some symptoms of being sick, you could tell you'd turned the corner, and soon would be well? Many people are able to reverse the onset of colds, flu, ear infections, eye infections, sore throats and many other types of illness by quantum jumping back to health. You can make use of a favorite placebo to assist you in these endeavors, such as drinking a steaming hot cup of honey-lemon tea, curling up in a cozy blanket to take a healing nap, or taking a hot bath with bath salts. Remember how you felt last time you got over something similar, and imagine you're feeling that way right now. Simply knowing you love and care for yourself can make a big difference in the time you spend feeling sick, and when you combine loving actions of self-care with an intention that you'd love to be well, you may well find your illness is very short-lived indeed.

One of the reasons that home remedies have been so effective for generations is that they consist mostly of what the first western doctors had at their disposal—lots of tender loving care and attention combined with good hygiene and common sense. Simply knowing that you care about your health and wellbeing, and that you're doing something nice for yourself can initiate huge healing changes inside your body. Give yourself inner smiles to whatever part of you is feeling injured or unhealthy, and get enough rest, drink enough fluids, wash your hands and face with soap, and gargle with salt water.

Harness the Placebo Effect in Daily Life

Once we understand that we are ascribing healing qualities to many people, things and activities in our lives, we can gain placebo effect benefits from things we do most every day. While eating fresh, seasonal, organic produce, we can tell ourselves, *"This food is helping me become healthy and strong."* When drinking glasses of water, we can tell ourselves, *"This water helps me improve the clarity of my thoughts."* Doing things we already suspect may help our health or cognitive abilities while taking a moment to appreciate such positive effects can help ensure we actually *do* feel healthier and smarter.

When we participate in regular exercise, we can assure we get the best results when we take a moment to appreciate the good we are doing for our body, mind, and spirit. By thinking to ourselves how we're getting stronger, more flexible, and increasing our endurance, we help make it so.

Whatever you are doing, you can improve your success and enjoyment by taking moments to think of and appreciate the expected and unexpected ways your life is now being improved.

If some things you do, such as eating candy or smoking, raise fears and concerns, you can do one of three things to reduce damage to your health and well-being. You can

(1) Minimize those activities in your life by stopping smoking, and reducing candy consumption,

(2) Tell yourself while engaging in those activities that these activities won't harm you in any way, and in fact are helping you be your healthiest and happiest, or

(3) Practice the meditative art of moving any worrisome thoughts to the periphery of your focus of awareness (don't overly think about it).

These are ways to address the pesky nocebo effect that can help minimize or completely eliminate any annoying negative side effects.

Ask How Good Can it Get?

Perhaps the greatest single lesson for all of us when reviewing the studies, experiences, and history pertaining to quantum jumping is that positive changes can arrive at any time. They can happen in an instant, and they can occur exactly when they're needed most. Such positive turns of events tend to arrive when we trust that they'll be there. This book contains a message of hope and numerous hands-on, practical exercises you can do to begin experiencing more positive quantum jumps in your life. Every human being deserves a life filled with laughter and love, and each of us has the power to help everyone —including ourselves—achieve it.

If you've ever noticed that when people experience a couple of unfortunate events, they sometimes ask, "What next?!" And often, very soon after asking such a question with its assumption that there's more bad news to come, something indeed goes wrong. When we flip that question around to its opposite, and genuinely and passionately desire to know just how good things can possibly get, it's possible to turn our attention and energy in a more positive and more enjoyable direction.

Today is the perfect day to ask in every situation, *"How good can it get?"* while intending that all obstructions to finding out be cleared away. If things are pretty much OK, yet you're not feeling enthusiastic or delighted, ask *"How good can it get?"* with an expectation that this question will receive a response. If you find yourself in a situation that is far from ideal, asking *"How good can it get?"* provides just the right catalyst to shift everything in a more positive direction.

Become the Change You Wish to See in the World

Whenever you make quantum jumps to realities you enjoy, rather than "manifesting" or bringing something into your life, you are actually *becoming* the change you wish to see in the world. The optimal quantum jumping mindset consists of staying focused on what you desire, and disregarding what's been bothering you. The essence of quantum jumping involves recognizing that there are many possible You's—and that you can access each and every one of the possible You's you'd love to be. With each quantum jump—with each change you make in yourself—everything around you changes, too. The energy required to get you from where you are now to where you'd like to be feels emotional—it feels like enthusiasm, like excitement, like enjoyment and gratitude and happiness. This requisite energy provides you with the bridge to the reality you're jumping into, so the higher your state of enthusiasm the better able you'll be to make the leap into a whole new wonderful world, and a whole new wonderful you!

Start by holding a vision of who you are in your preferred possible reality. Feel a sense of genuine excitement about living that life, and let the enthusiasm and rush of positive energy flow through you until you have goose bumps of joy. Then take some kind of action in keeping with who you are in your new reality, as you make a quantum jump to live the life of your dreams. Keeping a journal showing where you started from and the choices and actions you're taking along the way can give you a positive sense of progress on your journey.

Quantum Jumping in the Quantum Age

The dawning of this new Quantum Age is doing much more than bringing us quantum computers and quantum technologies... it's helping us understand our own quantum nature. Just as the first peoples of each continent knew and as the perennial philosophies taught, we are all interconnected— we are all as One. This starting point of awareness is akin to what physicists think of as quantum entanglement, and we feel the very real, palpable effects of this interconnectivity when we realize how much our relationships to one another and to Earth, the universe, and every living thing matter in our lives.

In this new Quantum Age, we recognize ourselves to be conscious reality shifters, choosing between many possible worlds. Just as quantum particles are considered to be either material particles at times, or as existing in pure energy form at other times, in the Quantum Age we begin to identify ourselves as sometimes being made of pure consciousness, and other times existing in form in physical bodies. Our conscious observer that we get to know through meditation and mindfulness practices discovers ourself existing in a superposition of states where we choose between numerous parallel universes of possibility—and understands that we are never as stuck, trapped or hopeless as we might at times imagine ourselves to be. The pure energy quality of our being-ness is akin to consciousness itself; it is a state of existence in which we select which material me's and you's we will be.

* * *

Thinking about the wide variety of amazing possible quantum jump experiences can leave us wondering what quantum jumps are like for people who try this, and what they've wished they knew along the way. We're most motivated to learn about various aspects of quantum jumping when we're getting started to make some jumps of our own, because that's when we find out there are a few more things we'd like to know.

The next and final chapter, *Making the Leap*, shares quantum jumping questions and answers from people who are quantum jumping. Sometimes there's nothing quite as useful as seeing someone's question in print that matches something you might be thinking. This question and answer chapter is full of interesting, practical and relevant aspects of quantum jumping that can help you with developing your quantum jumping skills.

Exercise:

Focus on Opportunities Rather than Problems

Think about something that hasn't happened yet that you fear might come true. Take a moment to get a clear sense of who and what are involved, and why, exactly, you feel concerned about this. Now think of a kind of person who would have very little trouble dealing with this particular scenario, and imagine what it would feel like to be this person with absolutely no fears about the matter, just going on with regular activities and feeling perfectly relaxed. Imagine you can see yourself benefiting from this exercise, and know that you are gaining new inspiration and strength to face whatever comes your way. Think of something wonderful that you'd really love to happen... and imagine how you'd feel if it really did happen to you. Imagine yourself being the person whose dreams are coming true... and know that just by contemplating it, you're inviting this possible reality to you.

Exercise:

Create Proactive Positive Stereotypes

Consider a goal you'd love to achieve that you feel some concern about actually being able to accomplish due to age, gender, education or experience. Tell yourself, *"Lots of people just like me are successful at this."* Every time you think of your dream, remind yourself of this again, and again, and again. Keep reminding yourself this is true, and that even if you don't personally know of such people, the multiverse is a mind-bogglingly huge place, and we can be fairly certain they are out there!

Exercise:

Remember How You Got Rich

Find a place and time where you can relax and concentrate quietly without being disturbed. Stretch your arms and legs and clear your mind, while breathing slow, deep, rhythmic breaths. Imagine you are meeting your best possible financially prosperous future self. Notice how this version of you looks, talks, dresses and thinks. Ask this possible future you how you got rich, and listen and watch carefully for any tips and clues you can observe. Thank your possible self for sharing these tips with you, and giving you a guiding hand forward into this prosperous future reality.

"The place where knowledge occurs
is the present.
That which recognizes the present
is mind."
— *Fred Alan Wolf*

Chapter 7

Making the Leap

Getting started with quantum jumping can literally be as simple as taking the first step forward in the direction of achieving one of your most cherished dreams—it's a matter of recognizing each opportunity that invites you to step into greatness, and say an enthusiastic *"Yes!"* to making the leap. Anyone who can relax, clear their mind, and envision bridging the gap to a desired reality can quantum jump. You've probably quantum jumped any time you've decided *"I'm done with this cold—I'm going to be just fine today,"* and every time you've leapt up out of bed despite wishing you could relax just a bit longer.

Because one of the best ways to learn is from example, this chapter includes a number of peoples' questions who've written to me about quantum jumping, along with my answers. You may well find that some of these questions and answers address something you're concerned about, or have been wondering about.

Many of these questions and answers will make a great deal more sense after you've done some quantum jumping, such as the questions about what to do if you find yourself having experienced another reality, but then bouncing back to where you started. Quantum jumping is a skill like anything else you learn to do, so the best way to improve is to get started and give it a try. If you feel inspired to keep a journal of your quantum jumping goals and experiences, that's a wonderful way to get and stay focused. When keeping a journal, you may find it helpful to record details surrounding each quantum jumping experience, such as what day of the week and time of day it is, how you're feeling physically, emotionally, and intellectually, and what's going on in your immediate environment.

If you've yet to try quantum jumping or any of the exercises at the end of each chapter, hopefully these questions and answers will provide you with confidence to stop waiting to try quantum jumping and go ahead and give it a go!

QUESTION: I'm pretty sure I quantum jumped, but not quite sure. Is there something that you can explain to me, how you know for sure?

ANSWER: Noticing significant changes in oneself, others, or one's surroundings can provide you with validation that you've made a quantum jump. Sometimes there isn't much discernible evidence of a quantum jump—particularly if the jump mostly affects your emotions, confidence, or other internal states of being. Sometimes the evidence of a previous reality vanishes during the jump, in such a way that X-ray photographs of a previously broken bone that is now suddenly healed, for example, can no longer be found.

QUESTION: Do you have to know how to do this to make it happen?

ANSWER: It helps to know it's possible to make a jump to another reality, and that such things happen often. The simple facts that the placebo effect is increasing its effectiveness ("sugar" pills are working better and better at providing positive effects for no apparent reason), and even when people know they are "just taking the placebo" are strong indicators that all most people really need is permission to know a huge positive change is possible.

QUESTION: Could a quantum jump actually happen the first time I try?

ANSWER: Yes, you can absolutely experience a quantum jump the first time you try. Most people find it helpful to know that reality shifts and quantum jumps happen frequently in lots of ways, so reading real-life, first-person accounts of such reality shifts and quantum jumps will definitely help. You can read many such stories in my book, "Reality Shifts: When Consciousness Changes the Physical World" and posted online in the "Your Stories" section of the RealityShifters web site.

QUESTION: Can you please help? I can't do it, and I feel like I've tried everything. What's the easiest and most effective way to quantum jump?

ANSWER: The easiest way to quantum jump is to DO something in keeping with the reality you're jumping to. For example, if you wish to be happier, smile for no reason. It's also important to be in a relaxed and energized state of mind, focused on your preferred reality. Such a mindset, in combination with believing you are in your desired reality, while doing things in keeping with staying there, helps ensure successful jumps.

QUESTION: I've noticed that sometimes I'll make a jump to a new reality, but then things revert back to the way they were before. Sometimes, this happens a few times. Is it possible to lock in a particular reality when you jump to one you like, or are these kinds of back-and-forth flip-flops part of the process?

ANSWER: Experiencing alternating realities indicates that additional energy is required in order to ensure a particular reality stays selected. Physicists observe electrons make quantum jumps from an initial ground state to an excited state when they absorb energy from photons to make that jump. These jumps occur instantaneously, as suddenly the electron is in a new orbit around the atomic nucleus. Because the excited state is not stable, at some later random moment, the electron may fall back to its ground state. For us to experience lasting quantum jumps in our lives, we need to become and stay energized, so we don't experience a reversion back to our previous state. Doing things to increase your energy, such as skipping, laughing, smiling, meditating, practicing qigong, and eating and sleeping well can help you "lock in" your quantum jumps.

QUESTION: I really need your help as I am experiencing something strange. Since quite recently I seem to be manifesting things kind of instantly. I don't know how it happened, but the most unthinkable has. Therefore, I am now not sure whether it is a quantum jump, a manifestation or if I am losing my mind! My life has got somewhat complicated as I now have an old love in my life after twenty-two years. Is this an alternate reality I am living in, or am I going crazy? Crazy as it may sound, I don't want to let go. I need to know: Are there any signs to prove I have indeed quantum jumped? Would there be physical changes that take place? I am having a voice change. Really strange, as this all happened around the same time. Is there any connection between instant manifestation and quantum jumping?

ANSWER: All manifestations can be viewed as being the result of quantum jumps to other universes of possibility that already exist... and instant manifestation is akin to making a quantum jump. Sometimes when one makes a jump, more than one reality shift might be observed in the leap into another parallel reality. Since we are constantly moving through parallel universes with every decision and choice we make, you could say with each new decision we arrive in a new alternate / parallel reality. When you notice something like a change in your voice, that provides you with further confirmation that you're in a new reality, just in case you were beginning to question your sanity. Often, there aren't lots and lots of signs you've made a jump, but rather small things you may or may not even really notice, that all taken together provide you with an unmistakeable sense of being in a whole new reality.

QUESTION: Cynthia, something happened that has happened several times before. I know that parallel universes exist. Last week, a friend and I went to the store and bought several bags of food. We were hanging around outside, feeding others who happened to come along. After everyone ate, my friend left along with everyone else. I took the remaining food (mostly candy bars, snacks, and other items) and put them into one of the plastic bags, throwing the leftover trash into a nearby waste can. One young man walked up and asked me if he could have something out of the bag and he took one thing (a Slim Jim beef snack) and left. I picked up the bag before he left, and put it over my shoulder, saying "Good night" to the guy and his friends, as I watched them leave the park. I was all alone in the park and I know that there was no one else around me or in the park (I was up against a short wall). I sat the sack down and smoked a cigarette, all the while looking at my surroundings. It was nighttime, but well lit in the area I was in. I was right beside

217

the sack the whole time. When I decided to get one of my candy bars out of the sack, I looked... and the sack had disappeared! I looked on the other side of the wall, and also checked the trash can to make sure that I had not mistakenly thrown it away even though I knew I didn't, because I had checked it for the contents after I had thrown the trash away. It was after 10pm, and there was no one else there for another fifteen minutes. I looked everywhere, and it was gone! Knowing that there was no way anyone could have taken that bag (on this plane anyway) the first thing that came to my mind was, "It's not in THIS universe or plane of existence anymore." This has happened when I am alone in my house with all the doors and windows locked and I know that I am not imagining anything. What do you think is happening?

ANSWER: Thanks for sharing your experience of the vanishing bag of food with me. This kind of reality shift does cause one to question what's going on when things vanish inexplicably like this. When we apply Occam's (or Ockham's) razor to this situation, we seek the simplest, least convoluted explanation for how your bag of food disappeared. Once you've ruled out theft or absent-mindedness, you can be nearly 100% certain that the bag literally vanished without human intervention. Since you've seen such things happen before when you've been alone in a house with locked windows and door, these incidents are not isolated, but are ongoing signs of something bigger going on. I've also experienced seeing things appear and disappear with no obvious physical cause. I propose that these kinds of reality shifts are indications that a quantum jump has been made in which the physical object in question is settling into a different location, in much the same way that quantum particles have been observed to blink on and off as they make quantum jumps. Just as physicists observing quantum particles blinking off call that time when the particle is gone a "quantum jump," so too can we occasionally observe

218

macroscopic physical objects, such as a bag of food, making quantum jumps. While this sort of quantum jump behavior is more frequently observed at the microscopic quantum scale, we can expect it to also occur at the macroscopic, human scale from time to time. One of the leading interpretations for quantum physics is the holographic multiverse model, in which there are many possible worlds accessible to each of us and everything and everyone. In this interpretation, there are many possible you's and many possible me's, and many possible bags of food. Thanks to our existing in a superposition of states (being simultaneously here and not-here) across many possible realities, we can expect to occasionally see evidence of quantum jumps occurring such as the one you've observed with your bag of food in the park.

QUESTION: What if a person wanted to use quantum jumping to become another Hitler, or something "bad"? Is that possible? In theory, one can use quantum jumping to change their life in any way they choose—not only for the better or good. As with any technology, it's not the technology that's evil, it's people who use the technology for evil.

ANSWER: Yes, people can make any kind of jump they wish, including choices they or others might later regret. This is why I recommend people set an over-riding intention of wishing the best for all concerned, rather than pushing forward with what seems to be a good idea at the time. :-)

QUESTION: What do you think of the concept of the "butterfly effect," in that small actions can have an accruemental effect? Does every decision we make move us into a different reality, and would parallel lives be in those realities where we made different decisions?

ANSWER: Every decision we make does indeed seem to move us into different realities within a vast realm of multiverse possibilities we can feel, intuit, dream, and directly experience. While it is true that our decisions and experiences naturally grow based on different series of actions we may take, there are many ways we can move or jump from one set of branching realities to another. You can think of it as being a little bit like the way a squirrel can jump between branches on a tree, finding several different paths along smaller branches to access the next large branch over. When we think of each of the larger branches representing something like choices in career paths, for example, we can imagine how we can make a leap from one career to another (from one big branch to another) at many different points in our lives.

QUESTION: I would appreciate if you could give me points on what I need to do in order to quantum jump. Does one have to meditate or are there other methods. Also, how would you know if you have done it? Love the subject. Please help me get started.

ANSWER: Meditation is a great way to quantum jump, but there are other methods. It's possible to feel grateful for what you desire, as a memory of something that's already happened. This is much like daydreaming, with the important difference that you'll be feeling the relaxed, happy memory of something having occurred, rather than connecting with the possible futures in which you're still hoping for something to change. The main idea behind making quantum jumps is that in order to live a different life, all you need do is first imagine it, then meditate silently and quietly until you attain a state of being detached from thoughts and feelings. When you sense a new connection to anther possible you living the life you'd prefer, immerse yourself naturally into that new state of being. And voilà! You've made a quantum jump. Life will likely feel pretty much the same, with similar daily activities, and any time you doubt or worry whether a change has occurred, return to a meditative state of quiet, and reconnect with the new reality you are selecting for yourself.

QUESTION: I just watched a video on You Tube from Abraham-Hicks, entitled: Is 2012 "the time of Awakening? " It's a short video, but in it she says (or Abraham says/suggests) that quantum leaping is not a good idea, because when you return you cannot keep up with the vibrational level. How does one maintain the vibrational level from quantum jumps?

ANSWER: It's important to set the intention to select over-riding intentions that realities you jump to will match energy frequencies you can hold and maintain. Working with one's high self... with super-consciousness... helps ensure success (rather than going with what ego seems to indicate we think we desire). When she says, "Quantum leaps are never a good idea" she's skipping past the concept that reality shifts are happening all the time. We see millions of shifts each day... millions of miracles... usually without noticing it. We don't notice them precisely because the energy DOES match, so leaps go unnoticed. Reality shifting masters—such as shamans, yogi, and masters—can easily maintain the energy levels required for all kinds of miraculous shifts. It takes time to build up to the energy levels required. I can agree with the art of allowing... the alignment process... that it takes time for most people through meditation to get to where they'd love to be.

QUESTION: Cynthia, I have been reading and watching loads of inspirational videos. Yours, Burt Goldman's and even Abraham Hicks. My biggest problem or block in my life is that I simply don't and can't feel joy or happiness. It's like a weight on my heart. I have no problems with my family. I own my own party store, that I am neglecting a lot. I am falling ill since of late, too. I just can't even smile. I do miss my earlier rather short relationship, but I have come to terms with it. Maybe there was a lesson to be learned in that. However, this lack of joy in my life is not recent, as it has been there for a long time. Like a heavy cloud of gloom constantly hanging over me. Do you think it could be a kind of psychological problem? I am looking at all angles and trying to clutch at anything as it feels awful living like this. An example would be of sitting in front of the TV, watching a hilarious comedy, and not finding it even amusing! What do you think?

ANSWER: Feeling happy and joyful helps bring more good people and experiences into your life, so it's important for you to start smiling and having fun again. A number of recent research studies indicate that there are some powerful, simple things you can do that can lift your spirits tremendously. Putting a pen in your mouth while turning the corners of your mouth up (simulating a smile) has been proven to lift people's spirits. Taking a few minutes at the end of each day to write down "What went well?" today—just the top three things—can effectively pull people out of the deepest, darkest funks. Behaving more like an extrovert by talking to more people is also proven to make people feel happier. And if for any reason you do find yourself ruminating over what went wrong instead of what went well, distract yourself by doing something fun that you enjoy. And if you're sitting in front of the TV watching comedy... put a pen in your mouth and turn the corners of your mouth up in a fake smile. If you're still not laughing at anything after a few minutes, turn the TV off, get up out of your chair and go do something fun with the person who deserves to be your best friend—you!

QUESTION: Because I learned about retrocausality from you through your videos, I'm indebted to your insight and wisdom which influenced my attracting your book, *Reality Shifts: When Consciousness Changes The World,* for Christmas. I'm now confident that our mental defaults that prevent the Law of Attraction from working for our benefit can be turned around into the security we need to avoid what we don't wish to attract...even if we're not entirely sure of what our genuine wishes are. Please share your thoughts on this.

ANSWER: The question about why do we sometimes not get what we set our intentions for, even when it seems to make no sense that our dream would be blocked is a question many people ask. It can feel especially discouraging to feel blocked from realizing a goal one has set one's sights with nothing else even coming a close second. In this modern age of so many people touting the ease and simplicity of the "law of attraction," it's easy to blame oneself for somehow having not correctly followed directions... yet that would be missing a very important point. When we recognize that all internal blocks, misgivings, lack of enthusiasm, missing out on being in the right place at the right time and knowing the right people are not mistakes, but instead can be viewed as our future selves retro-selecting reality paths for us, every so-called mistake and misstep can be viewed much more accurately and positively in a very different light. Just as we'd likely be happy later on to find out there was a good reason we didn't book passage on the maiden voyage of the Titanic, once we get sufficient distance to properly view all the events of our lives, we can see the value and wisdom of every "failure." When viewing one's life from the correct vantage point, failure is impossible.

QUESTION: Do things go missing in the other reality if I am successful at finding my lost things?

ANSWER: Things do not go missing in other realities when you find them arriving in your reality. What's actually happening is that you are the one moving between realities, and this is something you're doing all the time. We exist in a superposition of possible realities, choosing which reality we inhabit at every decision point. In most cases, the transition is so smooth that nobody gives it any thought... much the way frames of a movie progress forward with small movements, and everything seems perfectly natural. Except once in a while, something that wasn't there may suddenly appear, transport, or transform.

QUESTION: When a quantum jump to an alternate reality occurs, what happens to the "us" that is here in this reality? Does it die, enter a coma, disappear, or continue functioning at some other level? From your description, it sounds like it is our consciousness that actually jumps, not our body. Then I'm wondering what real effects quantum jumps have in this world.

ANSWER: That is an excellent question about what happens when we notice reality shifts or quantum jumps. It's such a good question because it gets straight to the heart of the matter of which theories are best at explaining what's happening in quantum physics. there are many different theories, and the parallel universes (Many Worlds) is one of them. According to the Many Worlds Interpretation of quantum physics, all of the possible realities fully exist. From my own direct experience with reality shifts and quantum jumps, I've found all the parallel realities to be equally real, with consciousness being the "traveler" between worlds. On occasions when I've jumped back and forth from one reality to another, such as one reality in which my neighbor's roof has leaf guards on the gutters, and another reality in which my neighbor's roof doesn't have leaf guards... everyone seems normal in both realities. The main effect, then, is that the traveler (consciousness) has memories of different realities.

QUESTION: If one is able to visualize a world and be in it through quantum jumping, what happens to the other individuals in the universe if that person puts them in that world?

ANSWER: From what the reality shifts and quantum jumps I've observed, it's clear to me that every person can conceivably access a universe unique to their own experience— while untold (perhaps infinite) other versions of themselves occupy other alternate universes with all the other people, making their own choices. I prefer to experience quantum jumps / reality shifts with others who also remember the way things used to be, rather than be the only one who is conscious of the change... but such shared recollections do not generally constitute the majority of quantum jumps / reality shifts. After most jumps / shifts, those who do not recall making a jump / reality shift continue on with their lives just fine, completely unaware of any changes whatsoever.

QUESTION: Is it necessary to remote view or otherwise fully envision a reality before successfully jumping into it? And if so, how does one best go about gaining such a vision?

ANSWER: While it's not necessary to obtain a remote view or premonitory vision of a possible reality before jumping into it, many such intuitions can provide a quantum jumper with a sense of activating or initiating such a jump. Sometimes what is seen is not a reality that is actually desired, and in such cases one's honest negative emotional energetic reaction is typically sufficient to vote against or deflect said jump. There is no one best way to gain visions of possible realities, but there are many types of meditations one can do that foster many-world-mindfulness. One can, for example, follow standard remote viewing (RV) protocol, with the target focus being that you see your best possible future some exact future point in time from now.

QUESTION: I once burned a DVD for my nephew that didn't burn properly for no apparent reason. It was what I call a convenience reality shift because at the time my nephew had a science project that required sacrificing a digital disc. So this defectively recorded DVD was available and he used it. What are your thoughts on reality shifts that spark convenience for individuals?

ANSWER: I believe these "shifts of convenience" happen much more often than most people realize... so that we're able to do things in accordance with our beliefs and preferences... even though at first take, it might seem things are starting to go wrong (such as a DVD not recording properly, thus wasting what seems like a perfectly good disc). Later, we find out that the "bad" news wasn't really bad news at all, but actually a wonderfully good turn of events, so we now have a sacrificial DVD disc we don't have to feel guilty donating to science. These sorts of things happen all the time, and it's my gut feeling that such synchronicity is a genuine indicator that consciousness is influencing the physical world.

QUESTION: I know that one can change the past by altering perception of it. So if we imagine the past differently, we'd be literally changing the past. But this is hard for me—it's like my subconscious mind doesn't believe it and rejects it.

ANSWER: Subconscious beliefs make a big difference in quantum jumping. We literally DO change the past every time we change our emotions about the past (such as feeling more gratitude). Starting a daily practice of meditation or prayer and sticking with it over time thus makes powerful changes in expectations about the past, which is the essence of quantum jumping and shifting reality.

QUESTION: I enjoy how you simplify quantum jumping. I am a little bit confused about when you write, "While to the universe, both of "you" still exist, usually your awareness of who you are will coalesce on one reality, leaving the other forgotten and left behind." If my awareness is in the "new reality," then what awareness is handling the old reality? And let's say I believe I may have quantum jumped out of a bad rollover accident on a highway going about 75 miles per hour. I remember becoming very relaxed and calm during the rollover, just observing what happens without fear—noticing the car rolling and ending up with my two infant children, myself, and the car unscathed. The insurance company records state I was on the phone when the accident occurred. I can attest that I was most surely not on the phone. It is all too mysterious for me. If I did quantum jump, how does that explain my children? Did they quantum jump?

ANSWER: Thanks so much for asking questions about (1) Who am "I" when jumping between realities? and (2) How do quantum jumps affect those around us?

The key to quantum jumping is actually very closely tied to how one identifies with oneself. There is a moment, when feeling supremely energized in which it's possible to feel a sense of oneness with all that is. In that moment of oneness, you might feel a sublime, timeless energetic experience of accessing all possibilities... including who you felt you were prior to this sense of oneness. All the possibilities can feel separate from this expanded sense of self because they are all limited possibilities. The awareness handling all possible realities resides fully in this feeling of unlimited, infinite oneness. The moment a particular reality is selected, the feeling of oneness is gone, to be replaced by consciousness of embodying one particular path in spacetime.

Quantum jumping affects those around us in interesting ways; sometimes we may not notice much of a change at all in other people, while other times we're aware of enormous transformations. When you and your children choose the same new reality as the one you select, you make a quantum jump together with a shared feeling of emotional, physical, and mental alignment regarding the reality you jumped from and the reality you jumped into. When your spouse selects different realities from the one(s) you prefer, it's possible to find you and your spouse literally moving in different realities so you feel an increasing sense of distance and separation emotionally, physically, and mentally from one another. It's also possible for two peoples' realities to temporarily separate for a while, and then to weave back together again later on. You can trust your intuition to inform you how close or distant you feel to those around you, and become more sensitive to the ways you are moving together or apart from those around you.

QUESTION: Do you know how Dr. Eben Alexander was able to cure himself while on the other side?

ANSWER: I'm fascinated by two recent authors and near death experiencers who cured/healed themselves while on the other side: Dr. Eben Alexander, author of *Proof of Heaven*, and Anita Moorjani, author of *Dying to Be Me*. Both of these people experienced a place of total love and no fear, in which all possibilities were viewable. Their experiences sound to me like something akin to being in a conscious state of pure energy, where all material possibilities can be seen and any one in particular can be chosen when the terminally ill individual chooses to return. With a majority of physicists now stating they believe that everything—including macroscopic size things like you and me—exist in a superposition of states, we can easily envision how we might be able to consciously realize what knowing of all those possible realities feels like during a near death experience. Dr. Eben Alexander and Anita Moorjani accessed states of lucid meditative consciousness which gave them a fresh sense of the possibility of returning to full and complete health, and those are the miraculously-healed realities each of them returned to, following their brushes with death.

QUESTION: I am one of the great number of people who have experienced a state of altered historical memories. Yes, Mandela was one, and I can remember actually seeing John F. Kennedy when I was young, alive. This, even though I was not born until June of 1964. I also recall RFK going on to win the Democratic nomination, before he was assassinated... not in a restaurant, but during a speech, outdoors.

But I think this is because I have shifted realities, somehow, several times in my life. The formula for my experiences is simple, really. Any time I have ever been near to death, or had a close call, reality changes. It's as though I died in one time line and then my consciousness jumped to a slightly different one, where I managed to pull through.

The changes can be gross or subtle. The last major difference was something that would have made news: the Hubble telescope was hit by something, a meteor or space debris of some kind, and went off-line, careening through space. This happened in 2009 or 2010. In 2010, I had a quadruple bypass, and died in recovery, to be later brought back and put in an induced coma for four days. After that, the changes started.

Earlier this year, I had minor surgery to put in two stents into blood vessels in my heart, and now my wife doesn't like cheese on her ham sandwiches, which she has loved for years. When I asked her about this, she said that it's always been that way. I was wondering if you have ever run into this sort of thing before.

ANSWER: Yes, I have heard similar stories from people who have undergone near death experiences and come back to life healed from supposedly impossible-to-heal-from afflictions. Many such miraculous cures can be attributed to making a leap of consciousness from one universe to another, so we subsequently witness altered histories and a variety of changes to what "has always been true." There appears to be something special about the way our consciousness operates in a near death experience that more readily allows us to make a jump from one reality to another as a vast array of possible realities open up and reveal themselves. People also experience increased shifts in reality and quantum jumps following lucid dreams, in which people know they are dreaming inside of their dreams, and realize the tremendous range of possible futures available to them.

QUESTION: I have been using a quantum jumping technique of lowering my brain waves, placing my intention for a twin self in a desired reality, going through a door, communicating with and merging with the other me and their frequency.. then bringing that energy back through the door into my life. It's so true that people with different aptitudes carry different frequencies. I can remember thinking and feeling, *"Wow! That's how it feels to be wealthy!"* or *"That's how it feels to play the piano really well!"* I've been thinking a lot about the infinite possibilities using that technique. I can try imagining it, but I don't know if I have advanced in my belief enough.

ANSWER: Yes indeed, there truly is a different energetic feeling and vibration to every possible "you" and each set of

231

skills and characteristics. Children and animals sense these inner 'vibes' readily, as this is there primary mode of connecting and communicating—and so it's possible to get re-sensitized to feeling the differences between each energy state and to harmonize with the sets of vibratory frequencies you most desire. It's quite a bit similar to the way stringed instruments at rest will vibrate in resonant harmony with other stringed instruments being played in a room. We can pick up a wealth of information in an instant through such harmonious resonant attunement of vibratory frequencies.

QUESTION: I have a question about changing the past. Recently a relationship of mine had gone terribly wrong and I believe it would be best for both of us involved (or at least me) to go back in time and change those events. Or even further to rewrite my high school history to make my parents proud and cause them less suffering through my adolescence. I want to create the reality I want to experience—and this would be the way. Is it possible? If so, how? Will imagining my desired past for five minutes every day help?

ANSWER: Thank you for your thoughtful and heartfelt question. Before making any suggestions, I advise you to carefully consider your reasons for wanting to change the past. Write down what it is that concerns you most, and get to the root of the underlying issue. This is essential, because each of us needs learning experiences in order to make "mistakes" and grow, and sometimes there is grace and beauty in remembering reasons not to be or do what we've been and done in the past.

Rather than envisioning a particular preferred past, you'll likely experience best results by feeling grateful and appreciative for a preferred present and future. While it is possible for you to have a different past, your memory of what happened is likely to remain the same. This is how it feels when people experience spontaneous remissions of disease, for example, as they remember they used to have cancer, and now it's gone.

You can think of where we are right now in this present moment as a convergence of many possible pasts and many possible futures. In actuality, everything on Earth including you exists in a superposition of states... which means there are many possible you's and many possible me's. Whenever we focus with clear intent on an adjacent reality with sufficient energy (drawn from inner Qi energy from practicing qigong, meditation, breathing exercises, yoga, etc), we can make a jump from one reality to another. As we move to an adjacent reality in which we feel more committed to being the kind of person we wish we were, for example, we increase the likelihood that we are now connected with a different set of histories.

QUESTION: So I cannot change past events or anything then? I am a bit confused.

ANSWER: You can definitely change the past, just not so easily in the way you might have seen it depicted in books, movies, or TV shows. Rather than literally going back to the past to interact with people, places and events, the kind of changing-the-past that happens more commonly (the kind everyday people do all the time) involves a process of:

- Imagine many possible pasts, presents and futures existing
- Envision a parallel world you'd like to be living in now
- Raise your Qi through qigong, meditation, yoga, or prayer
- Behave as if you're in a parallel world you'd like to be in

The process outlined above enables you to make a leap from one possible reality to another, in a way that will likely also alter

233

the past. What you are most likely to notice is a change in the way you interact with others and the way you now embody qualities you most admire right now in the present time.

Some people have traveled back in time, but I have not yet heard of any consistent, reliable process by which this can easily be achieved.

QUESTION: Many years ago, I worked with a very good female friend who was in a marriage that wasn't working for her. Our relationship was purely platonic. One day, we had lunch together in the cafeteria and she asked me if I ever thought about what would have happened if we had met before she met her husband. I was completely stunned by this question, as it came out of the blue. I knew at the time I was in love with her, but never told her that, or gave any hints. On our way back to work, I walked her down the hall to her office. We got to the stairwell where I would go down to my basement office, and said goodbye. When I opened the door, I was surprised to see her enter the stairwell with me, and just stood there, dumbfounded. At that point, she reached up and began to kiss me. All I can remember after our lips barely touched is that instantly I was at the bottom of the stairs looking up at her—I mean INSTANTLY. She was standing at the top of the stairs with a Cheshire Cat smile. I was disoriented and confused. How did I get to the bottom of the stairs? What had happened during and after the kiss? We never spoke of the kiss and a while later I moved, and we lost contact. I have since heard of people who were instantly transported to different locations to avoid accidents. I wonder if that is what happened to me. Is there another universe with me remembering the kiss? Are there universes with us married happily or unhappily? How do I find out?

234

ANSWER: I have also heard accounts of people teleporting to safety, and perhaps that is what happened to you that day. Scientists know that plants and animals have quantum properties—that we are quantum beings—and in this sense, just as plants try out all possible paths before choosing the best one to bring energy from sunlight through their leaves, it's likely that human beings also try out many pathways where each choice transports us to other universes of possible realities. In this universe, you and your friend are not together. In another, you are married. In yet another, you were together and then broke up. With each choice representing a branching point into further universes of possibility, there likely is at least one in which you remember the kiss. You can practice meditation quantum jumping techniques to imagine you are now in a reality where you remember that kiss... and in a meditative state something akin to hypnosis, you can see and feel and know what actually happened that day so many years ago.

QUESTION: So if it is possible to change the past with quantum jumps, the version of me who was really happy would swap with me, or he dies?

ANSWER: Rather than so strongly identifying with any one particular possible 'you,' think of the *real* you as being the consciousness inside of yourself. Next, imagine that just as a child might leap from stone to stone crossing a stream, you can jump from reality to reality. The other possible you's each live out their various lives, and you (the consciousness that is truly you) are free to move between them. Changing the past as you make jumps between possible realities happens as a natural process, because each parallel possible world has its own unique alternate history.

QUESTION: I was wondering when someone quantum jumps if the reality that gets shifted into ours is reverted to the one we are trying to shift. In other words, if I were trying to heal my severely asthmatic lungs, would some other 'me' be afflicted with the condition I was healed from?

ANSWER: When someone quantum jumps to a healthier situation, such as if you were healing severely asthmatic lungs, you can think of what is occurring as your consciousness moving from one possible you (the one with asthma) to another possible you (one of many possible you's who do not suffer from asthma). This kind of leap is therefore not so much affecting the other possible you's as your conscious awareness of which of the many possible you's you are. Another way to view this hypothetical example is that while to your perspective, your physical condition and physical reality have changed, both possible you's still exist—you've just moved from considering yourself one into considering yourself to be another.

QUESTION: The later part of last month I took garlic bread with cheese out of the oven and burned the ends of the three last fingers of my right hand. It hurt real bad. I went forth and carefully attended to making dinner and setting the dinning room table for all of us to eat. I had to wake up very early to get Richard off to the airport. Returning back home and taking to bed again. I woke up happy and feeling good. Showering is where I noticed the burns had completely healed. I walked downstairs and showed my mother. She thought it was great and commented that I always was a fast healer. A couple weeks or more had passed, when again in the shower I noticed the burn returned just on my pinky finger (baby finger). It was all bubbled up at the end, and it surprised me. It was after a lucid dream, and my body and mind felt "plugged in" as my energy was so high. I showed my mom and she thought it was strange. I

236

showed Richard later that day and he did not know what to make of it. I thought to myself how it is healed and how it will just be renewed, healed. I had an underlying fear that other burns might come back, as my body felt on fire. I quickly tossed these thoughts away knowing "I'm good, healthy and well." The "fire" feeling subsided and quickly left as I realized this fire energy was not going to manifest my old wounds of history. The finger burn washed away and left only an outline of a heart shape for a day. Then all was like new, without a trace of burn. Any ideas about why this type of reality shift would occur?

ANSWER: From a perspective of making a quantum jump from one reality to another parallel world, it's our consciousness that is making the jump from one universe to another, and through our consciousness we sometimes go back and forth between parallel universes, before settling into one that best suits our intentions and energy levels. A jump from one reality to another requires attaining a meditative detached state of awareness, and in order to reach and stay in a reality we best enjoy, it's helpful to keep our intention and energy levels at that sufficiently high level. An example of how these intentions, energy levels and beliefs manifest in terms of reality selection can be seen in scientific evidence from longitudinal studies of people with different beliefs about a group of people such as the elderly, for example. Prejudices about a group of people we don't (yet) belong to are particularly interesting, as people subsequently move into that group as they age, making these kinds of studies truly fascinating. It turns out that scientific studies are showing that we become what we believe. People who believe, for example, that elderly people are mentally and physically slow, less competent, and prone to illness and disease... tend to suffer from exactly what they expect to suffer from, whereas those who view the elderly as wise, healthy, strong, resilient, flexible, respected, powerful, and courageous tend to become exactly that. Any areas where we experience vacillation is an indicator to us, therefore, of beliefs we can change in ourselves, and provides us with a kind of compass to improving the overall positive trajectory of our lives. Reality shifts for the most part occur "Be Cause," which is to say that the whole point is to get us to become aware of how we are able to make leaps from sick to healthy... and sometimes back to sick again. We are living in a truly amazing time in history when the placebo effect is becoming twice as powerful as it was just a few decades ago, as people increasingly become aware that healing is a natural process, and we can make a leap to being well. Keeping your sense of identity attuned with the highest level of your consciousness—with what you might call your spirit, high self, or soul—can result in the most consistently positive reality shifts.

QUESTION: I have a very interesting question for you that I really hope you may have some insight about. Last night we had yoga class and we were working on the 7th body (the aura). Our instructor was in bad shape, but came to teach anyway. Her health has not been good for years and has gotten worse recently. We have gotten really close and she has told me the story about her health. She has tried many healers and doctors over the years with minimal effects. I could tell by how she was teaching class last night that she was really not well. At the end of class while we were lying in Shavasana, she and her ride left, and another woman in class took over. We did our final meditation and then before we wrapped up, we did a mini healing session for our instructor. While we were doing this, tears ran down my face. My heart just aches for her. Another woman in class who I know pretty well was visibly upset also. When I got home, I still had to do my daily practice, since I hadn't had time to do it that morning. Afterward, I sent our instructor some distance Reiki. I was so exhausted that I passed out as soon as I went to bed. Here is where things got strange. In the middle of the night I started to wake up, as I always do, but there was a tone playing so loudly in my ears that it seemed like it was coming from inside. I was half out of it, so I just relaxed into it, even though I was aware. It just kept playing and playing, and it sounded exactly like a Tibetan Singing Bowl. I fell asleep with that vivid image and sound in my head. I started dreaming about playing one and hearing that sound. I don't remember the details of the dream, but our instructor was in it and said that they are incredibly healing. So my question is... Any idea why that would happen or what the significance could be? It was really loud and I clearly heard and felt the sound. I would appreciate any insight.

ANSWER: I am certain your connection to your instructor is a powerful one, capable of helping her heal through your close association and love for her. Yes, Tibetan Singing Bowls can be incredibly healing, when they assist people in accessing a level of relaxation mentally, physically, and emotionally that transcends physical bounds... thus granting people access to jumping into a reality of full and complete health. From the stillness and relaxed timeless center of consciousness one enters when hearing Tibetan Singing Bowls, it's possible to remember that we are always and ever at the center of many possible realities, and it's possible through the higher level of energy felt with its associated freedom from pain and fear to make the jump to a parallel universe in which we are healthy. Your ability to hear Tibetan Singing Bowls and your emotional and energetic connection to your instructor can be very healing for her, due to the fact that you and your instructor can experience a kind of entanglement that readily transfers the healing state of mind you are experiencing to her, along with the healing benefits.

QUESTION: I need your help. My last quantum jump was great. But all too soon, things went sour and the person who came into my life isn't even talking to me anymore. Now I am finding it difficult to cope as I was so happy earlier and now am so down and depressed. Please advise me how I can get back. Can quantum jumping work in that manner? Can I go back and maybe change things that happened or can I have a new quantum jump with the same individual? I have tried to quantum jump again but now it isn't working. What am I doing wrong?

ANSWER: I sense this is a time when you are feeling conflicted, which is leading to your current dissatisfaction. I recommend starting by asking yourself what would make you truly happy, and making time to relax and clear your mind—to meditate. If the person who came into your life is pivotal to your happiness. you can envision the reality where you are happy together. By envisioning that possible reality and gaining advice, support, and energy from who you are in that reality, you can become the woman who is with the man of your dreams. If when you meditate and clear your mind you see that your happiness lies in another direction, fully visualize yourself in that other reality, and gain the advice, support and energy from that possible you.

QUESTION: When I jump, I get really tired, disoriented and dizzy for a few days. Do you have any tips for controlling that and making my jumps smoother?

ANSWER: You can reduce the disorientation, dizziness, and exhaustion by imagining that the energy center above your head is filled with light, like a pillar of golden white light and that this is where your consciousness is centered. Maintain a sense that this is the real and true you, and that you in the form of pure consciousness is the one enjoying visits to other realities via quantum jumps. Keeping this focus of your identity can greatly reduce adverse effects.

QUESTION: I have a question about my mom. If you have an answer I'd love to read it. I'm in my late 50's and this situation occurred back in my 20's. I was in my mom's bedroom talking to her. All of my life she always seemed strong and extremely confident about everything in her life. Anyway, she was on the floor in front of an end table, when all of a sudden she said things like *"I can't do this,"* and *"I don't have a clue what I'm trying to do in this life."* This moment of doubt and confusion literally lasted for just about 40-60 seconds. Have you ever heard of or read of anything like this before? I was extremely shocked when it first happened, and I'm still very confused.

ANSWER: I've heard from people who've been startled by moments of feeling suddenly quite different from their usual character and demeanor, like a sense of sudden joy or hopelessness washed over them. Some highly intuitive people, like myself, sometimes pick up these feelings from someone we dearly love who is going through a life trauma or transition, such as dying or attempting suicide. I've felt feelings of intense joy at the moments some of my dearest friends and family members have passed away, as if I was sharing in the ecstatic part of their death experience. I've also felt inexplicably sad and hopeless when dear friends of mine were contemplating suicide. It's also possible that sometimes a person might become aware of a parallel reality in which they are feeling suddenly quite different.

QUESTION: Is it possible to make a psychic/mental connection to someone from another universe and time (another point in space-time) that is not an alternate version of yourself both temporarily or permanently? If this is possible, how could one do that?

ANSWER: Yes. Sometimes such connections happen in what we think of as our reality when two people are literally experiencing different realities concurrently—existing in two separate parallel worlds. You might notice this happening when a friend or loved one insists you said something you know you didn't say, for example—or when they remember something completely differently than you recall for that particular sequence of events.

QUESTION: Is it possible to imagine future events for yourself and still have them occur in your future instead of your present or past?

ANSWER: Yes, it's possible to get such a clear sense of 'future memory' as if you're absolutely certain of the way things are about to unfold, and then have them occur pretty much exactly as you'd foreseen.

QUESTION: How would you suggest to someone who is new to this whole thing and/or a skeptic, but who wants to learn how to do these things to train their mind to doing the correct focus of attention and sense of all things being possible, and also get past all doubt?

ANSWER: I recommend that skeptics do their best to keep an open mind. Think of techniques for working with consciousness as a kind of internal technology that works a bit like placebos. Placebos can still be wildly effective, even when people know they're "just getting the placebo," provided people also know that for some reason, placebos often work as well or even better than other treatments.

QUESTION: I want to shift to a better job. I meditate, focus on what I want (love, happiness, success), live the feeling for a long time and let go by making myself busy—basically doing what it takes to quantum jump. but until now, no change?

ANSWER: Visualize yourself doing the things in your new life associated with what your new job duties will be, and how your life will be different once you have a better job. Be so fully in the mindset of being that person-with-the-wonderful-job that you truly *are* that person. Behave like that version of you in how you dress, how you talk, how you spend free time, how you think, how you dream and how you feel. Imagine that person-with-the-wonderful-job is helping you right now to make your dream of the perfect job come true. Know this connection will help you get and stay on track to becoming that person-with-the-wonderful-job.

*   *   *

Next Quantum Steps... and Jumps

The dawn of the new Quantum Age invites us to keep an open mind to what we've previously considered to be possible and impossible. Humanity has reached an exciting point in which it's becoming increasingly clear that we are not constrained by one single history, nor do we all even recall having shared exactly the same past. We are equally free to experience a multitude of possible now's and a vast expanse of unlimited possible futures. In this new Quantum Age, we can best help one another and ourselves by getting and staying energized and relaxed, while imagining and envisioning better possibilities.

We've learned a great deal about how it feels to live in a superimposed state by reviewing first-hand accounts including medical histories of those who've witnessed healing changes in their lives. We've seen how witnessing alternate histories need not merely cause confusion, but can foster confidence in the glorious flexibility and diversity of this resilient, mysterious multiverse. We've considered a new way of viewing the many worlds we live within, with newfound appreciation for how everything can change in an instant when we make a quantum jump.

While this chapter contains a broad assortment of questions and answers about quantum jumps, as you get started quantum jumping, you may well have further questions that weren't covered here. You can get answers to these questions, so write them down in a journal or notebook, and set out to find the answers. Make use of the exercises at the end of each of the chapters in this book, and point at your head to stimulate clearer thinking. Most people find that simply asking the right questions at the right time is the most important thing, because the questions you ask focus your attention on what you most wish to know, which in turn prepares you to see the answers to your questions when they arrive.

My favorite question is simply, *"How good can it get?"* which is appropriate to every situation, no matter how apparently innocuous or troublesome it might at first appear. Open-ended positive questions like this one invite good energy and inspiration to help with what is currently transpiring... and such assistance is always a good thing. You don't need to say this question out loud, either. Just thinking it can make a tremendous difference in the most surprising and amazing ways, by virtue of training your attention in positive directions.

Your continuing commitment to practicing the exercises in this book on a regular basis can help you become a better quantum jumper. Please take a few minutes when you finish reading this book to write down some exercises you can start doing on a regular basis to keep practicing quantum jumps. While ideas are still fresh in mind, this is the perfect time to write a note you can put on your refrigerator, desk, wallet or some other place you'll regularly see it to remind yourself of simple ways to improve your life.

As Benjamin Whichcote pointed out, *"There is no better way to learn than to teach."* Since this subject of quantum jumping interested you enough that you've read all the way through this book to the very last page of the last chapter—I hope you will take every opportunity to expand your comprehension of quantum jumps by sharing ideas from this book with others. Talking about quantum jumps and asking people questions about quantum jumps will help you more fully understand the topic. The scientific studies and quantum jump stories in this book are excellent conversation starters for discussions with friends, colleagues and family.

Most of all, remember that every moment is brimming over with possibilities. Remember that there are many possible you's, and by simply focusing your attention and awareness on the ones you'd most like to be, you're halfway there. One of the best ways to gain access to your favorite realities and live the life of your dreams is to keep asking, *"How good can it get?"* and get ready to find out!

Exercise
Increasing Energy Meditation

One of the best ways to ensure once you've jumped to a higher-energy reality that you can stay there (and not snap back and forth, or end up where you started) is to increase your Qi, or internal energy. Many meditation masters explain that newborn infants come into this world with a great deal of Qi, and you can see babies and infants breathing directly to their "ocean of Qi" just below their navels. This is an exercise you can do to increase your internal energy, and keep your energy levels high.

(1) Place the palm of your hand on your lower abdomen so the thumb rests atop your navel and your other fingers are below.

(2) Inhale full and complete breaths all the way to your lower abdomen, so your hand rises as you breathe in.

(3) Relax your muscles as you exhale fully in a slow outward breath. Continue breathing out even after you feel you've exhaled all the air from your lungs.

(4) Continue breathing slowly, deeply, and fully with the slowest natural count of inhalation and exhalation.

(5) See if you can lengthen the time of inhalations from your natural slow, steady count (such as four seconds) to something even slower but still comfortably doable for you (such as six seconds).

(6) Close your eyes, clear your mind, continue relaxing your muscles and keeping your breathing slow, deep, and steady for the next ten to twenty minutes.

Notes

WELCOME TO THE QUANTUM AGE

Lobello, Carmel. "What is a Quantum Computer—and Why Does Google Need One? These Almost Unfathomably Futuristic Machines Can Run More Calculations in an Instant than there Are Atoms in the Universe." *The Week*. 20 May 2013.

Larson, Cynthia. *Reality Shifts: When Consciousness Changes the Physical World*, 2011.

1. EXPERIENCING THE QUANTUM REALM

Planck, Max. "Das Wesen der Materie (The Nature of Matter)" speech at Florence, Italy, *Archiv zur Geschichte der Max-Planck-Gesellschaft*, 1944, Abt. Va, Rep. 11 Planck, Nr. 1797.

Reyes, Jeanette. "Tornado Survivor Jumps from Ten Foot Boulder with Baby to Take Cover," *KATV ABC7*, 12 April, 2013.

Gleick, James. "Physicists Finally Get to See Quantum Jump with Own Eyes," *New York Times*, October 21, 1986.

Webb, Richard. "First Quantum Effects Seen in Visible Object," *New Scientist*, 17 March 2010.

James, William. *The Principles of Psychology, Volume Two*, Henry Holt and Company, New York, New York, 1918, pp. 524-525.

Feinberg, Cara. "The Placebo Phenomenon: An Ingenious Researcher Finds the Real Ingredients of 'Fake' Medicine." *Harvard Magazine*, Jan-Feb 2013.

Kaptchuk, Ted J. et al. "Placebos Without Deception: A Randomized Controlled Trial in Irritable Bowel Syndrome." *PLoS One*, 5(12). 2010. e15591.

Park, Lee C., and Uno Covi. "Nonblind Placebo Trial: An Exploration of Neurotic Patients' Responses to Placebo When Its Inert Content is Disclosed." *Archives of General Psychiatry*, April 1965, Vol. 12, pp. 336-345.

Decher, David. "Ten Crazy Facts About the Placebo Effect." *Listverse*, 16 February 2013.

Spiegel, Alix. "The Growing Power of the Sugar Pill." *National Public Radio (NPR)*, 8 March 2010.

Conzemius, Michael G. and Richard B. Evans. "Caregiver Placebo Effect for Dogs with Lameness from Osteoarthritis." *Journal of the American Veterinary Medical Association*. 2012; 241(10). pp. 1314-1319.

Scudellari, Megan. "Worried Sick: Expectations Can Make You Ill. Fear Can Make You Fragile. Understanding the Nocebo Effect May Help Prevent this Painful Phenomenon." *The Scientist*, 1 July 2013.

Enck, Paul, and Winfried Hauser. "Beware the Nocebo Effect." New York Times, 10 August 2012.

Roberts, Michelle. "'Most Family Doctors' Have Given a Patient a Placebo Drug." BBC News, 20 March 2013.

Taylor, Ashley. "How Faith Can Affect Therapy." *New York Times*, 10 July 2013.

Rosmarin, David H., Joseph S. Bigda-Peyton, Sarah J. Kertz, Nasya Smith, Scott L. Rauch, and Thröstur Björgvinsson. "A Test of Faith in God and Treatment: The Relationship of Belief in God to Psychiatric Treatment Outcomes." *Journal of Affective Disorders*, 2012.

Kirkley, Alexandra et al. "A Randomized Trial of Arthroscopic Surgery for Osteoarthritis of the Knee," *New England Journal of Medicine*, 2008:359; 1097-1107.

Dierdich, NJ and Goetz CG. "The Placebo Treatments in Neurosciences: New Insights from Clinical and Neuroimaging Studies," *Neurology*, 2008; 71(9):677-684.

Weger, U., and Loughnan, S. "Mobilizing Unused Resources: Using the Placebo Concept to Enhance Cognitive Performance." *The Quarterly Journal of Experimental Psychology*, 66(1), 23-28, 2013.

Pham, Lien B. and Taylor, Shelley E. "From Thought to Action: Effects of Process-Versus Outcome-Based Mental Simulations on Performance," *Personality and Social Psychology Bulletin*, 25/1999; pp. 250-260.

Adam, Hajo and Galinsky, Adam. "Enclothed Cognition." *Journal of Experimental Social Psychology*. 10.1016/j.jesp.2012.02.008.

Bousso, Raphael and Leonard Susskind. "The Multiverse Interpretation of Quantum Mechanics." *Physical Review D 85.4*, 2012.

Kaku, Michio. *Physics of the Impossible: A Scientific Exploration into the World of Phasers, Force Fields, Teleportation, and Time Travel*. Doubleday. New York, New York, 2008.

Dossey, Larry. *The Power of Premonitions: How Knowing the Future Can Shape Our Lives*. Dutton, Penguin Group, New York, New York, 2009.

Kastner, Ruth. *The Transactional Interpretation of Quantum Mechanics: The Reality of Possibility*. Cambridge University Press, 2012. pp. 154-160.

Merali, Zeeya. "Back from the Future," *Discover*. April 2010.

Jahn, R.G., B.J. Dunne, R.D. Nelson, Y.H. Dobyns, and G.J. Bradish. "Correlations of Random Binary Sequences with Pre-Stated Operator Intention: A Review of a 12-Year Program." *Journal of Scientific Exploration*. 11, no. 3. (1997), pp. 345-367.

Leibovici, Leonard. "Effects of Remote, Retroactive Intercessory Prayer on Outcomes in Patients with Bloodstream Infection: Randomised Controlled Trial." *British Medical Journal* 323, no. 7327 (2001). 1450.

Popescu, Sandu. "Viewpoint: Weak Measurements Just Got Stronger. In the Weird World of Quantum Mechanics, Looking at Time Flowing Backwards Allows Us to Look Forward to Precision Measurements." *Physics* 2, number 32. 27 April 2009.

Hosten, O. and P. Kwiat. "Observation of the Spin Hall Effect of Light via Weak Measurements." *Science* 319 no. 5864. Feb 2008. pp. 787-790.

Dixon, P. Ben, David J. Starling, Andrew N. Jordan, and John C. Howell. "Ultrasensitive Beam Deflection Measurement Via Interferometric Weak Value Amplification." *Physical Review Letters* 102, no 17 (2009): 173601.

2. WHY DO WE QUANTUM JUMP?

"From the Big Screen to the Soccer Field," *CUNY, 30* November 2012.

Lobello, Carmel. "What is a Quantum Computer—and Why Does Google Need One? These Almost Unfathomably Futuristic Machines Can Run More Calculations in an Instant than there Are Atoms in the Universe. " *The Week.* 20 May 2013.

Wolchover, Natalie. "New Physics Complications Lend Support to Multiverse Hypothesis," *Scientific American,* 1 June 2013.

Ball, Philip. "Hawking Rewrites History... Backwards. To Understand the Universe We Must Start from the Here and Now." *Nature.* 21 June 2006.

Taylor, Rosie. "Is Our Universe Merely One of Billions? Evidence of the Existence of 'Multiverse' Revealed for the First Time by Cosmic Map." *Mail Online.* 19 May 2013.

Berezhiani, Zurab and Fabrizio Nesti. "Magnetic Anomaly in UCN Trapping: Signal for Neutron Oscillations to Parallel World?" *The European Physical Journal C.* 72(4). 2012. pp 1-7.

Burton, Robert A. *On Being Certain: Believing You Are Right Even When You're Not.* St. Martin's Press. New York, New York. 2008. pp. 9-12.

Neisser, U., and Harsch, N. "Phantom Flashbulbs: False Recollections of Hearing the News About *Challenger," Affect and Accuracy in Recall: Studies of "Flashbulb" Memories.* Cambridge University Press. New York, New York. 1992. pp 9-31.

Palmer, Jason and Mansfield, Alex. "Quantum Biology: Do Weird Physics Effects Abound in Nature?" *BBC News,* 27 January 2013.

Jabr, Ferris. "Jailbreak Rat: Selfless Rodents Spring Their Pals and Share Their Sweets." *Scientific American,* 8 Dec 2011.

Bao, Xiao-Hui Bao, Xiao-Fan Xu, Che-Ming Li, Zhen-Sheng Yuan, Chao-Yang Lu, Jian-Wei Pan. "Quantum Teleportation Between Remote Atomic-Ensemble Quantum Memories." *Proceedings of the National Academy of Sciences,* 109.50, 2012. pp. 20347-20351.

Hildner, R., D. Brinks, J.B. Nieder, R.J. Cogdell, N.F. van Hulst. "Quantum Coherent Energy Transfer over Varying Pathways in Single Light-Harvesting Complexes." *Science,* 2013; 340 (6139): 1448.

ICFO-The Institute of Photonic Sciences. "Uncovering Quantum Secret in Photosynthesis." *ScienceDaily*, 20 June 2013.

Griffin, Catherine. "Stable Quantum Teleportation: Breakthrough in Teleporting Information Between Gas Clouds." *Science World Report*, 7 June 2013.

Gane S, Georganakis D, Maniati K, Vamvakias M, Ragoussis N, Turin L, et al. "Molecular Vibration-Sensing Component in Human Olfaction." *Plos One*, 25 Jan 2013, 8(1): e55780. doi:10.1371/journal.pone.0055780.

Sheldrake, Rupert. *Dogs Who Know When Their Owners Are Coming Home: And Other Unexplained Powers of Animals.* Random House, 2000.

Backster, Cleve. *Primary Perception: Biocommunication with Plants, Living Foods, and Human Cells.* White Rose Millenium Press, Anza, California. 2003.

Keim, Brandon. "Everywhere in a Flash: The Quantum Physics of Photosynthesis." *Wired*, 3 March 2010.

Ball, Phillip. "The Dawn of Quantum Biology." *Nature*, Vol 474, 16 June 2011.

Lambert, Neill, Yueh-Nan Chen, Yuan-Chung Cheng, Che-Ming Li, Guang-Yin Chen and Franco Nori, "Quantum Biology." *Nature Physics, 9*, 10-18, 9 December 2012.

Turin, Luca http://www.bbc.co.uk/news/science-environment-21150046

Larson, Cynthia. *RealityShifters Guide to High Energy Money.* 2010.

Atwater, PMH. *Future Memory.* Carol Publishing Group, 1996, New York, NY, pp. 23-24.

Vedral, Vlatko. "Living in a Quantum World." *Scientific American*, June 2011, 304, pp. 38-43.

Herr, Eva. *Consciousness: Bridging the Gap Between Conventional Science and the New Super Science of Quantum Mechanics.* Rainbow Ridge Books, Faber, VA, 2012, pp. 22-24.

Ball, Phillip. "Experts Still Split About What Quantum Theory Means." *Nature*, 11 January 2013.

Dossey, Larry. *The Power of Premonition: How Knowing the Future Can Shape Our Lives.* Dutton, New York, NY, 2009, p 137.

3. CHANGING PAST, PRESENT & FUTURE

"Brain Oscillations Reveal We Experience the World in Rapid Snapshots." *SciTechDaily,* 14 May 2012.

Romei, Vincenzo and Joachim Gross, Gregor Thut. "Sounds Reset Rhythms of Visual Cortex and Corresponding Human Visual Perception." *Current Biology,* Volume 22, Issue 9, 8 May 2012, pp. 807-813.

LaFee, Scott. "Cause and Defect." *U-T San Diego,* 22 June 2006.

Sheehan, Daniel P. *Frontiers of Time: Retrocausation - Experiment and Theory. AIP Conference Proceedings.* Melville, New York, *2006. Vol. 863.*

Miller, Carolyn. *Creating Miracles: Understanding the Experience of Divine Intervention.* H.J. Kramer, 1995.

Newmark, Thomas. "Cases in Visualization for Improved Athletic Performance." *Psychiatric Annals,* October 2012. 42(10). pp. 385-387.

Lenzer, Jeanne. "The Body Can Beat Terminal Cancer—Sometimes." *Discover Magazine,* 21 August 2007.

O'Regan, Brendan, and Caryle Hirshberg. "Spontaneous Remission." *An Annotated Bibliography.* Sausalito, California, USA, Institute of Noetic Sciences, 1993.

Larson, Cynthia Sue. *How Do You Shift Reality? Survey,* realityshifters.com, April 2000.

Waugh, Rob. "Inception Becomes Reality: People Can Teach Themselves New Skills in Dreams." *Daily Mail,* 22 December 2011.

Waggoner, Robert. *Lucid Dreaming: Gateway to the Inner Self.* Moment Point Press, Needham, Massachusetts. 2009, pp 240-243.

Erlacher, Daniel. "Practicing in Dreams Can Improve Your Performance." *Harvard Business Review,* April 2012.

Falloon, Katie. "Flying Through the Catacombs." *Yale Daily News,* 22 February 2012.

Atwater, PMH. *Future Memory.* Carol Publishing Group. 1996, New York, NY, pp. 28-31.

4. QUANTUM JUMP EXPERIENCES

Hodgson, Sarah. "'I'll Never Forget It': Manchester Remembers Tragic Woolworths Fire that Claimed 10 Lives in Blaze." *Mancunian Matters,* 9 May 2013.

Lee, Gary Yia and Nicholas Tapp. *Culture and Customs of the Hmong.* Greenwood, 2010, p. 154.

Eldred, Sheila A. "Telepathy Between Couples: Is It Real?" *Discovery Magazine,* 12 Feb 2013.

Washington, Denzel. *A Hand to Guide Me: Legends and Leaders Celebrate the People Who Shaped Their Lives.* Meredith Books, Des Moines, Iowa, 2006.

Johnson, Melissa. "First Step in Becoming a Winner: Act Like One." *New York Times.* 20 March 2009.

Powell, Alvin. "Coach Turns Fight for Life Into Lesson." *The Harvard University Gazette.* 2 March 2000.

Diliberto, Gioia. "Patience Worth: Author from the Great Beyond." *Smithsonian,* September 2010.

Worth, Patience. *The Sorry Tale.* Forgotten Books, May 2012.

Holt, Henry. "A Nut for Psychologists." *The Unpartizan Review.* Vol. XIII, January-April 1920, pp. 357-372.

Moorjani, Anita. *Dying to Be Me: My Journey from Cancer, to Near Death, to TrueHealing.* Hay House, 2012, p. 135.

Chumley, Cheryl K. "'Angel' Priest Mysteriously Appears At Near-Fatal Accident Site, Helps Victim," *The Washington Times.* 8 August 2013.

Sleczkowski, Cavan. "Mystery 'Angel' Priest Appears At Missouri Car Crash, Performs 'Miracle,' Then Disappears." *The Huffington Post.* 8 August 2013.

Miller, Carolyn. *Creating Miracles: Understanding the Experience of Divine Intervention.* H.J. Kramer, Inc. Tiburon, CA, 1995.

Kaku, Michio. *Physics of the Impossible: A Scientific Exploration into the World of Phasers, Force Fields, Teleportation, and Time Travel.* Doubleday. New York, New York, 2008, p 306.

Heath, Pamela Rae. *Mind-Matter Interaction: A Review of Historical Reports, Theory and Research.* McFarland. 2011, p 29.

Janvier, Thomas A. "Legends of the City of Mexico," *Harper's Magazine.* 1909. Volume 118, pp. 63-66.

Steiger, Brad. *The Reality Game and How to Win It: Making the Mysteries of Time and Space Work for You.* California Newcastle Publishing Co, 1986.

5. GET A QUANTUM JUMP START

Murten, Robert King. *Social Theory and Social Structure.* Free Press. 1964.

Lyubomirsky, Sonja, Laura King, and Ed Diener. "The Benefits of Frequent Positive Affect: Does Happiness Lead to Success?" *Psychological Bulletin.* Vol. 131(6), November 2005, pp. 803-855.

Nolen-Hoeksema, Susan, B.E. Wisco, and Sonja Lyubomirsky. "Rethinking Rumination." *Perspectives on Psychological Science.* 90, 2006. pp. 692-708.

Seligman, Martin EP, *Flourish: A Visionary New Understanding of Happiness and Well-Being."* Free Press, Simon & Schuster. New York, New York, April 2011, p. 43.

Strack, Fritz et al. "Inhibiting and Facilitating Conditions of the Human Smile: A Nonobtrusive Test of the Facial Feedback Hypothesis [Attitudes and Social Cognition]." *Journal of Personality and Social Psychology, May* 1988, v. 54, pp. 768-777.

Soussignan, Robert. "Douchenne Smile, Emotional Experience, and Autonomic Reactivity: A Test of the Facial Feedback Hypothesis." *Emotion,* Vol 2(1), Mar 2002, pp 52-74.

Rodriguez, Tori. "Botox Fights Depression." *Scientific American Mind.* August 2012.

Fitzgerald, Kelly. "Botox Injections Can Make You Depressed." *Medical News Today.* 13 April 2013.

Finzi, Eric, and Erika Wasserman. "Treatment of Depression with Botullnum Toxin A: A Case Series." *Dermatologic Surgery.* May 2006. Vol 32(5). pp. 645-650.

Fleeson, William, Adriane B. Malanos, and Noelle M. Achille. "An Intraindividual Process Approach to the Relationship between Extraversion and Positive Affect: Is Acting Extraverted as 'Good' as Being Extraverted?" *Journal of Personality and Social Psychology.* December 2002, 83(6), pp. 1409-1422.

Reddy, Sumathi. "How an Introvert Can Be Happier: Act Like an Extrovert." *Wall Street Journal,* 23 July 2013.

Gale, Catharine R., Tom Booth, René Mõttus, Diana Kuh, Ian J Deary. "Neuroticism and Extraversino in Youth Predict Mental Wellbeing and Life Satisfaction 40 Years Later." *Journal of Research in Personality,* 2013. 10.1016.

Zelenski, John M., M.S. Santoro, and D.C. Whelan. "Would Introverts be Better Off if they Acted More Like Extraverts? Exploring Emotional and Cognitive Consequences of Counterdispositional Behavior." *Emotion.* April 2012, 12(2), pp. 290-303.

"Extrovert Teens 'Happier Adults': Study." *Daily Telegraph,* 18 July 2013

Lambert, Craig. "The Psyche on Automatic." *Harvard Magazine.* November-December 2010.

Carney, Dana R., Cuddy, Amy J.C., Yap, Andy J. "Power Posing: Brief Nonverbal Displays Affect Neuroendocrine Levels and Risk Tolerance." *Psychological Science.* 2010, 21(10), pp. 1363-1368.

Cuddy, Amy JC, Caroline A. Wilmuth, and Dana R. Carney. "The Benefit of Power Posing Before A High-Stakes Social Evaluation." *Harvard Business School Working Paper,* No. 13-027. September 2012.

Cuddy, Amy JC and Maarten W. Bos. "iPosture: The Size of Electronic Consumer Devices Affects Our Behavior." *Harvard Business School,* Working Paper 13-097, 20 May 2013.

Grabmeier, Jeff. "Study: Body Posture Affects Confidence in Your Own Thoughts." *Ohio State University Research News.* 5 October 2009.

Briñol, P., Petty R.E., and Wagner B. "Body Posture Effects on Self-Evaluation: A Self-Validation Approach." *European Journal of Social Psychology.* 25 February 2009; 39. pp. 1053-1064.

Graham, Judith. "Older People Become What They Think, Study Shows." *The New York Times.* 19 December 2012.

Levy, Becca R., Martin D. Slade, Terrence E. Murphy, and Thomas M. Gill. "Association Between Positive Age Stereotypes and Recovery from Disability in Older Persons." *The Journal of the American Medical Association.* 21 November 2012, Vol. 308, No. 19. pp. 1972-1973.

Levy, Becca R. "Mind Matters: Cognitive and Physical Effects of Aging Self-Stereotypes." *The Journals of Gerontology.* 3 February 2003. Volume 58, Issue 4. pp. P203-P211.

Levy, Becca R., MD Slade, SR Kunkel, and SV Kasi. "Longevity Increased by Positive Self-Perceptions of Aging." *The Journal of Personal and Social Psychology.* August 2002. 83(2). pp. 261-270.

Vince, Gaia. "Ease Pain by Taking a Good Look at Yourself." *New Scientist.* 1 November 2005.

Lewis, Jennifer S., Karen Coales, Jane Hall, and Candida S. McCabe. "Now You See It, Now You Do Not: Sensory-Motor Re-Education in Complex Regional Pain Syndrome." *Hand Therapy,* 2011. 16:29.

McGonigal, Kelly. "Hugging Yourself Reduces Physical Pain." *Psychology Today.* 21 May 2011.

Gallace A, Torta DM, Moseley GL, Iannetti GD. "The Analgesic Effect of Crossing the Arms." *Pain.* June 2011; 152(6): 1418-23.

Friedman, Ron and Andrew J. Elliot. "The Effect of Arm Crossing on Persistence and Performance." *European Journal of Social Psychology.* 38(3), 2008. pp. 449-461.

Hutson, Matthew. "Clenching Your Fists Increases Willpower: Steely Muscles Can Lead to Steely Resolve." *Psychology Today.* 10 April 2011.

Hung, Iris W., and Aparna A. Labroo. "From Firm Muscles to Firm Willpower: Understanding the Role of Embodied Cognition in Self-Regulation." *Journal of Consumer Research.* 2011, Vol 37(6). pp. 1046-1064.

Brown, Kristen V. "How Posture Influences Mood, Energy, Thoughts." *San Francisco Chronicle.* 3 September 2013.

Peper, Erik and Lin, I-Mei. "Increase or Decrease Depression: How Body Postures Influence Your Energy Level." *Biofeedback.* Fall 2012; 40(3): 125-130.

Berry, Sarah. "Fake It 'Til You Make It In Love." *Sydney Morning Herald.* 7 November 2012.

Wrenn, Eddie. "Why Acting Like You Are in Love Can Lead to the Real Thing," *Daily Mail,* 4 July 2012.

Alleyne, Richard. "Watch Out Lotharios: Faking Romantic Feelings Can Actually Lead to the Real Thing." *Daily Telegraph,* 4 July 2012.

Epstein, Robert. "How Science Can Help You Fall in Love." *Scientific American Mind,* January/February 2010, pp. 26-33.

Kamenica, Emir, Robert Naclerio and Anup Malani. "Advertisements Impact the Physiological Efficacy of a Branded Drug." *Proceedings of the National Academy of Sciences of the United States of America,* 31 August 2010.

Bailey, Sebastian. "Get Smarter—Point to Your Head (Yes, Really)." *Forbes,* 25 July 2013.

Fetterman, Adam K., Michael D. Robinson. "Do You Use Your Head or Follow Your Heart? Self-Location Predicts Personality, Emotion, Decision-Making, and Performance." *Journal of Personality and Social Psychology.* Vol. 105(2), August 2013, pp. 316-334.

Atasoy, Ozgun. "Your Thoughts Can Release Abilities Beyond Normal Limits." *Scientific American.* 13 August 2013.

Langer, Ellen, Maja Djikic, Michael Pirson, Arin Madenci and Rebecca Donohue. "Believing is Seeing: Using Mindlessness (Mindfully) to Improve Visual Acuity." *Psychological Science.* 2010. Volume 21, number 5. pp. 661-666.

"Believing is Seeing: How Mindset Can Improve Vision." 2 May 2010. *PhysOrg.*

Bates, William H. *The Bates Method for Better Eyesight,* Holt. 1981.

Schneider, Meir. *The Handbook of Self-Healing: Your Personal Program for Better Health and Increased Vitality.* Penguin Books. 1994.

257

6. QUANTUM JUMPS IN DAILY LIFE

Atwater, PMH. *Future Memory*. Carol Publishing Group. 1996, New York, NY, pp. 23-24.

Hölzel, Britta K., James Carmody, Mark Vangel, Christina Congleton, Sita M. Yerramsetti, Tim Gard, Sara W. Lazar. "Mindfulness Practice Leads to Increases in Regional Brain Gray Matter Density." *Psychiatry Research: Neuroimaging.* 30 January 2011. Vol. 191, Issue 1. pp. 36-43.

Boyce, Christopher J., Alex M. Wood, and Nattavudh Powdthavee. "Is Personality Fixed? Personality Changes as Much as "Variable" Economic Factors and More Strongly Predicts Changes to Life Satisfaction." *Social Indicators Research* 111.1 (2013). pp. 287-305.

Rodriguez, Tori. "Life Satisfaction Linked to Personality Changes." *Scientific American Mind,* July 2013.

Jackson, Joshua J, Patrick L Hill, Brennan R. Payne, Brent W. Roberts, and Elizabeth A.L. Morrow. "Can an Old Dog Learn (and Want to Experience) New Tricks? Cognitive Training Increases Openness to Experience in Older Adults." *Psychology and Aging.* Vol 27(2), Jun 2012, pp. 286-292.

Segerstrom, Suzanne C. *Breaking Murphy's Law: How Optimists Get What They Want from Life—and Pessimists Can, Too.* The Guilford Press. 1 September 2007.

Manning, Craig. *The Fearless Mind: Five Essential Steps to Higher Performance.* Cedar Fort, Inc. 8 January 2010.

Beilock, Sian. *Choke: What the Secrets of the Brain Reveal about Getting it Right When You Have To.* Atria Books. 2011.

Reynolds, Gretchen. "Phys Ed: Why Exercise Makes You Less Anxious." *The New York Times.* 18 November 2009.

McGreal, Scott A. "Internet Ranting and the Myth of Catharsis: Why Ranting and Venting are Terrible Ways of Handling Anger." *Psychology Today.* 28 March 2013.

Martin, R.C., K.R. Coyler, L.M. VanSistine, and K.L. Schroeder. "Anger on the Internet: The Perceived Value of Rant-Sites." *Cyberpsychology, Behavior, and Social Networking.* Feb 2013. Volume 16, Number 2. pp. 119-122.

Bushman, Brad J. "Does Venting Anger Feed or Extinguish the Flame? Catharsis, Rumination, Distraction, Anger, and Aggressive Responding." *Personality and Social Psychology Bulletin.* June 2002. Volume 28, number 6. pp. 724-731.

Graham, J.E., M. Lobel, R.S. DeLuca. "Effects of Written Anger Expression in Chronic Pain Patients: Making Meaning from Pain." *Journal of Behavioral Medicine.* June 2008. Volume 31, Number 3. pp. 201-212.

Larson, Cynthia. *RealityShifters Guide to High Energy Money.* 2010.

Edmonds, Caroline J. and Denise Burford. "Should Children Drink More Water? The Effects of Drinking Water on Cognition in Children." *Appetite,* Vol 52(3), June 2009, pp. 776-779.

Draxler, Breanna. "Your Brain Calls in Backup to Find Lost Things." *Discover,* 22 April 2013.

Heath, Pamela Rae. *Mind-Matter Interaction: A Review of Historical Reports, Theory and Research.* McFarland. 2011, p 95.

7. MAKING THE LEAP

Wolf, Fred Alan. *Parallel Universes.* Touchstone. New York, NY, 1988.

Larson, Cynthia. *Reality Shifts: When Consciousness Changes the Physical World.* 2011.

Larson, Cynthia. http://realityshifters.com/pages/yourstories.html

Alexander, Eben. *Proof of Heaven: A Neurosurgeon's Journey into the Afterlife.* Simon and Schuster. 23 October 2012.

Moorjani, Anita. *Dying to Be Me: My Journey from Cancer, to Near Death, to TrueHealing.* Hay House, 2012, p. 135.

Larson, Cynthia Sue and Anne Menne. "When Worlds Collide: How Parallel Realities Can Heal Interpersonal Relationships." *Proceedings of the 21st International Conference on the Study of Shamanism and Alternative Modes of Healing.* 6 September 2004.

Angus, Joseph. *The Handbook of Specimens of English Literature.*

Index

J

Jackson, Joshua, 189

Jahn, Robert, 43

James, William, 22-23, 82

Jesus Christ, 128-129

Josephson junction, 18

K

Kennedy, John "Jack", 56, 122, 230

Kennedy, Walter, 28

Kwiat, Paul, 43

L

Labroo, Aparna, 166-167

Langer, Ellen, 173

Large Hadron Collider (LHC), 52

Leibovici, Leonard, 43

Levy, Becca, 161-162

Lewis, Michael, 153

life satisfaction, 154, 188

lose weight, 34, 67

Loughnan, Stephen, 33

lucid dreaming, 11, 45, 65, 72, 85, 87, 90, 101-105, 111, 231, 236

Lyubomirsky, Sonja, 149

M

Manning, Craig, 193

Mason, Peggy, 59

McCabe, Candida, 163-164

McCabe, Randi, 30

magnetic resonance imaging (MRI), 89-90

magnetoreception, 62

Many Worlds Interpretation (MWI), 38-39, 41, 52-53, 225

Matzke, John, 93-94

meditation, 45, 79, 87, 91-92, 101, 111, 125, 144, 150, 183-187, 191, 198, 208, 221-222, 226-227, 233, 235, 238, 246

melanoma, 93

Mersini-Houghton, Laura, 55

meta-awareness, 104

Miller, Carolyn, 134

mindset influences visual acuity, 173

mirror neurons, 59

mirrors reduce pain, 163-164

money, 70, 198-199

Moorjani, Anita, 133-134, 229

Morgan, Peter Thomas, 104-105

Mosely, J. Bruce, 31-32

muscle-firming, 166-167

symbolic meaning of clothing,
34-35

synchronicity, 8, 11, 96, 98, 105,
145, 227

T

telepathy, 85, 120-121

teleportation, 10, 36, 38, 58, 60, 63,
71, 73-74, 94, 141

The Kid, 107

The New York Times, 17, 128

The Sorry Tale, 128-130

The Time Machine, 83

Thomas, Billy, 123

Thut, Gregor, 83

time symmetry, 43, 84, 203

time travel, 142

top-down cosmology, 54

transactional interpretation, 38,
41-44, 83, 106

tunneling, 10, 36-37, 51, 53, 58, 63,
66, 74

Turin, Luca, 63-64

U

unable to breathe, 69

uncomfortable position, 166-167

unpleasant taste, 166-167

V

venting anger, 196-197

vision improvement, 173-174

visualizing the process, 34

W

Waggoner, Robert, 102-103, 105

warts, 32

Washington, Denzel, 49, 123-124

Weger, Ulrich, 33

weight loss, 34, 67

Wells, H.G., 83

what went well exercise, 150-151,
175, 223

willpower, 3, 68, 166-167

Wisconsin Card Sort Task, 105

Wiseman, Richard, 168-169

Wollmer, Axel, 153

Wolf, Fred Alan, 212

Worth, Patience, 127-131

Wray, Nelda, 31

X

X-ray, 94, 131-132, 214

Y

Z

About the Author

Cynthia Sue Larson is a transformational speaker, best-selling author, and life coach whose passion is inspiring people to become conscious reality shifters. Cynthia has been featured in numerous TV and radio shows, and her favorite question in any situation is, *"How good can it get?"* Cynthia received a BA degree in physics from UC Berkeley and an MBA degree from San Francisco State University, and her popular *RealityShifters* newsletter can be subscribed to at: **www.realityshifters.com**

Made in the USA
Columbia, SC
06 March 2024

32675977R30157